Inflammable Material

Kevin C. Dunn

BLOOMSBURY ACADEMIC
NEW YORK · LONDON · OXFORD · NEW DELHI · SYDNEY

BLOOMSBURY ACADEMIC
Bloomsbury Publishing Inc, 1359 Broadway, New York, NY 10018, USA
Bloomsbury Publishing Plc, 50 Bedford Square, London, WC1B 3DP, UK
Bloomsbury Publishing Ireland, 29 Earlsfort Terrace, Dublin 2, D02 AY28, Ireland

BLOOMSBURY, BLOOMSBURY ACADEMIC and the Diana logo are
trademarks of Bloomsbury Publishing Plc

First published in the United States of America 2026

A catalog record for this book is available from the Library of Congress.

ISBN: PB: 979-8-7651-3324-8
ePDF: 979-8-7651-3326-2
eBook: 979-8-7651-3327-9

Series: 33 1/3

Typeset by Deanta Global Publishing Services, Chennai, India
Printed and bound in the United States of America

For product safety related questions contact productsafety@bloomsbury.com.

To find out more about our authors and books visit www.bloomsbury.com
and sign up for our newsletters.

Contents

Acknowledgments — viii
Preface — x

1   Belfast, Punk and the Troubles — 1
2   From Highway Star to Stiff Little Fingers — 17
3   The Singles: "Suspect Device" and "Alternative Ulster" — 33
4   The Songs of *Inflammable Material* in the context of the Troubles — 57
5   After Lighting the Match: SLF's troubled relationship with Belfast punk — 77
6   Punkwashing: The Legacy of SLF and Punk in Belfast — 107

Notes — 117
Bibliography — 134

Acknowledgments

This book is informed by years of research on punk in general and Belfast punk in particular. During multiple trips to Belfast, I was fortunate to interview numerous punks, artists, activists, and academics. Too many, it turns out, to include them all in this book. My appreciation and respect go to all of those who spoke with me. In particular, I would like to voice my enormous gratitude to Brian Young, Petesy Burns, Greg Cowan, Henry Cluney, Terri Hooley, and Stuart Bailie. My friends in Ireland have been an important part of this project, with special thanks to John Brady, Verena Commins, Nessa Cronin, Louis de Paor, Jim Donaghey, Méabh Ní Fhuartháin, Debbie Lisle, Michael Lydon, Mick McCann, Anna McCarthy, and Evan O'Connor. In the US, the *Razorcake* familia remain a vital source of support, especially Todd Taylor, Daryl Gussin, Donna Ramone, Michael Fournier, Mike Faloon, Jennifer Whiteford, and Kayla Greet. I am also especially thankful to Chuck Crews, Lisa Gibson, Steve Mank, Nick Ruth, and Mike Schill for seeing this project to completion in various ways. I was extremely lucky that Sean Carswell, Henry Cluney, Mike Faloon, Mike Fournier, Todd Taylor, and Brian Young were willing to read the manuscript, in parts or its entirety. The book was greatly improved by their insights and corrections, but ultimately all mistakes are mine. Thanks to Sarah Piña and the staff at Bloomsbury Press, especially Leah Babb-Rosenfeld. Finally, enormous thanks to Anna, Barrow, and Strummer, my essential co-conspirators and supporters, without whom I would be so much the lesser.

This book does not pretend to be a definitive history of the Stiff Little Fingers. That would be Roland Link's excellent *Kicking Up a Racket*. Moreover, this book only scratches the surface of Northern Ireland's complex history and the importance of the Belfast punk scene. I encourage anyone interested in either of those topics to consult the bibliography and explore the various works listed there. My gratitude goes to all those scholars, journalists, and writers whose work I have drawn from.

Preface

Inflammable Material, the debut album by Stiff Little Fingers, became the first independent LP to reach the UK Top 20. Released by Rough Trade in 1979, the album immediately won widespread acclaim. Calling it a "remarkable document" upon its release, Paul Morley of *NME* enthused: "as astonishing in its impact as *The Ramones*, *Inflammable Material* is the classic punk rock record."[1] The album's vitality and urgency largely reflected the context from which it emerged. The band hailed from Belfast during a time when Northern Ireland (also known as Ulster) was gripped by "the Troubles," an era of political violence that eventually claimed more than 3,500 lives over three decades. Released after the first decade of the Troubles, the album's thirteen tracks capture the band's spirited and reflexive tales of sectarian violence, teenage angst, doomed romance, police brutality, crushing boredom, and the banality of everyday life, even in a conflict zone.

In his biography of the band, Roland Link writes that *Inflammable Material* was "A true punk rock album made by a true punk rock band, from the perfect punk environment, and if that wasn't enough, it had been released on a truly independent label."[2] The cover featured nine gray fire symbols laid out in a three-by-three grid against a stark black background with the name of the band and album spelled out in red letters that looked pasted on and just slightly out of alignment.[3] While other punk albums of the time (such as The Clash's debut and the Sex Pistols' *Never Mind the Bollocks*) evoked a handmade ethos while still exuding stylized chic, *Inflammable Material* literally wore its authentic DIY scrappiness on its sleeve.

This book examines the context of *Inflammable Material's* creation and release as part of the emerging Belfast/Northern Ireland punk scene in the late 1970s. First and foremost, the album was a product of, and response to, the Troubles, the era of bombings, assassinations, random terrorism, and armed repression involving the British Army, the police, and competing paramilitary forces. The Troubles defined every aspect of life in Northern Ireland from the late 1960s until the 1998 Good Friday Agreement established a precarious peace. *Inflammable Material* offered sonic documentation of that time from the perspective of the terrorized youth navigating brutal sectarian divisions. The members of Stiff Little Fingers helped establish the Belfast punk scene that emerged in the midst of the Troubles—a scene since celebrated as an example of average people defying the violent social divisions of their everyday life and forging alternative visions of the future. As this book illustrates, Belfast punks created important non-sectarian spaces in which social networks were built, alternative ways of being were imagined, and campaigns of political and social activism were realized, eventually helping make the peace process a reality. A core argument of this book is that the Belfast punk scene, of which the Stiff Little Fingers were founding members, was politically important. Or, as journalist Stuart Bailie, author of *Trouble Sings: Music and Conflict in Northern Ireland*, put it, "it's fair to suggest that scores of people in Northern Ireland owe their lives to a bunch of scratchy, shouty tunes."[4]

For many, *Inflammable Material* represents *the* defining document of the emerging Belfast punk scene of the 1970s. The band had formed only two years earlier, releasing their first single in February 1978 on their own Rigid Digits label. "Suspect Device" represented a blistering anti-authoritarian screed aimed at all sides of the conflict in Northern Ireland. The single so appealed to influential BBC radio DJ John Peel that he played it repeatedly on his show for weeks, leading to a distribution deal with the emerging independent record label Rough Trade. The band's second single, "Alternative Ulster," is generally regarded as the definitive statement of punk's political potential in challenging the status quo and offering alternative visions of the future. Both singles were included on *Inflammable Material*, an LP that contained further tracks challenging the stultifying sectarianism gripping Northern Ireland at the time. Still heralded as one of the greatest punk albums of all time, *Inflammable Material* is a testament to the power of punk as a social force.

Punk Matters

Punk proved to be more than just a passing musical fad. Since its development in London and New York, punk offered individuals around the globe resources for participation and access in the face of the alienating process of modern life. At its core, punk provides the opportunity for disalienation and personal empowerment, which can become deeply political acts.[5] In the context of 1970s Belfast, punk explicitly promoted political and cultural empowerment for a population that had been marginalized and terrorized for years.

For most of us, politics and economics appear as distant, uncontrolled, alien forces, constituted in everyday life by the separation of the specialized activities of professionals and intellectuals from the residue of everyday life in work, family, and leisure. Before the emergence of punk, for example, rock bands typically played in concert halls separated from the audience in ways that reinforced the "rock star" myth. For many, punk offered an attractive alternative. Reflecting on punk's initial emergence, Matt Davies noted, "Punks strove to eliminate the distinctions between performers and audience and did so by a radical form of egalitarianism: anyone could be a punk, and any punk could play in a band or, if they preferred, to publish a zine, to organize shows, or to produce or distribute records."[6]

By its very nature, punk reflects an anti-status quo position, a reactive response to the injustices of the world. And for punks in late 1970s Northern Ireland, there were plenty of injustices to respond to. As Brian Young, guitarist of Rudi, the first punk band in Belfast, observed, "Part of punk's appeal was its questioning of the status quo. And in Northern Ireland, we had a lot to question."[7] What often made punk's anti-status quo disposition so politically impactful was its linkage to the do-it-yourself (DIY) ethos.[8] In this vein, Brian Young also noted,

> By necessity, Ulster punk was DIY all the way, kick-started by a handful of semi-delinquent and disgruntled teens who were plain pissed off and had the grit, spunk and determination to go out and do something about it! . . . Unlike the UK and US prime movers, most all of the bands were still teenagers and almost without exception this was the first time we'd ever set foot on a stage.[9]

Punk can also be proscriptive, not just reactive. Through its employment of the DIY ethos, punk offers a guide for action and self-empowerment. Instead of passively accepting the world as it is, punk inspires people to do something about it on a *personal* level. Don't wait for someone else to fix what bothers you—do it yourself. By embracing DIY strategies, punk provides both an active rejection of the way things are, questioning the naturalness of the social order, while also calling alternative ways of thinking and living into being. For punks in Northern Ireland, this process meant imagining and striving for an "Alternative Ulster."

Part of punk's political impact involves the ways in which it helps produce *oppositional identities*. In the terms of cultural theorist Dick Hebdige, the oppositional identities produced within punk scenes represent a "disruptive noise" that challenges the "naturalness" and "inevitability" of the accepted orders in society.[10] Punk enables individuals to construct alternative forms of identity that are in opposition to societal norms and their underpinning political and economic practices.[11] As this book will examine, punk could generate dangerous and revolutionary acts in the context of the violent sectarianism permeating Northern Ireland during the Troubles.

Of course, individuals do not exist in vacuums but are part of larger social groupings. For this book, I talk of the Belfast punk scene as the collection of like-minded individuals who came together in an "affective alliance."[12] This book examines the ways in which these individuals created a scene in Belfast and how that scene evolved. The book will pay particular attention to the significant political and social work accomplished by the scene within the violent context of Northern Ireland. Central to the telling of this story is the complicated relationship between the Stiff Little Fingers and the scene they helped create.

Outline of Book

The Stiff Little Fingers and their debut album were very much a product of and response to their historical moment, and it is hard to appreciate either without an understanding of Northern Ireland's complicated history. Therefore, the first chapter offers a brief historical discussion of British settler colonialism in Ireland, the creation of Northern Ireland as a separate political entity, the eruption of the Troubles, and the emergence of punk. The second chapter narrates the evolution of the band itself, from their roots as a teenage hard rock cover band to their conversion to punk and fateful run-in with two journalists. The third chapter focuses on the band's first two singles—"Suspect Device" and "Alternative Ulster"—with an eye on how their direct and critical engagement with the Troubles led to the band's growing notoriety at home and abroad, culminating in the release of their debut album. The fourth chapter unpacks the album, critically examining all thirteen songs of *Inflammable Material* while discussing their origins and intentions. Chapter five explores the importance of the Belfast punk scene, the difficult relationship between the band and that scene, and the evolution of both after the release of *Inflammable Material*. The book concludes with a discussion of the ways in which the band and the scene are being memorialized in modern Belfast.

1
Belfast, Punk, and the Troubles

This book is about the city of Belfast in Northern Ireland, the punk scene that emerged there, four young men who helped spawn that scene, and their debut LP, which is still considered one of the greatest punk albums ever made. But first, it is useful to start with a simple question, whose answer is incredibly important to everything that follows: why is there a Northern Ireland?

British Settler Colonialism in Ireland

England is rightfully regarded as one of the most aggressive imperial powers of the last millennium.[1] As they proudly proclaimed, "The sun never sets on the British Empire." What is possibly less well known (unless you are Irish) is their use of Ireland as a laboratory for their colonial project. Having originally established control over much of the island after the twelfth-century Anglo-Norman invasion, the English enacted a variety of practices and policies they would subsequently utilize around the world. These colonial practices included the creation of plantations and export crop-based economies, as well as encouraging settler colonialism and labor migration, to say nothing of institutionalized violence and repression. These actions, which would characterize the British Empire from North America to Africa and Asia, were all implemented first in Ireland. Ireland served as the proto-colony upon which the British Empire was built.

There isn't space to cover the entirety of the 800 years of British colonial rule in Ireland, but a few key narrative points are important for our story.[2] In Ireland, the British employed the practice of settler colonialism, just as they would in places such as North America, Australia, New Zealand, South Africa, and (to a lesser extent) Kenya. This practice entailed encouraging the emigration of British citizens to a colony, where they would enjoy significant power and privilege over the indigenous population. In Ireland, this emigration created a social hierarchy that became generational. After several decades, descendants of settlers felt they had claims to the land and a sense of belonging in the same ways descendants of settlers in North America do today. These Anglo-Irish soon dominated most aspects of life in Ireland. The indigenous population, generally known as Gaelic Irish, were disadvantaged politically, economically, and socially in myriad ways, effectively having few rights.

Several historical events are worth flagging. In the early sixteenth century, the English King Henry VIII created the Anglican Church and, after an armed reconquest of Ireland, proclaimed himself King of Ireland in 1542. While his actions meant England was effectively a Protestant nation, most Gaelic Irish remained Catholic. Soon afterward, England began establishing plantations across Ireland, involving the confiscation of Gaelic Irish-owned land and the increased settlement by emigrants from England and Scotland. The government enacted these practices to control and "civilize" the Gaelic Irish, which often meant to "Anglicize" them in terms of language, religion, and culture.

Land confiscation and resettlement began during the 1550s but picked up speed under King James I in the 1610s with the creation of the Ulster Plantations as the crown seized lands across the north of Ireland. New settlers mostly came from northern England and the Scottish Lowlands. These emigrants were overwhelmingly Protestant. Tensions erupted in 1641 with the outbreak of a rebellion aimed at restoring land and political power to the Irish Catholic gentry. Soon afterward, the English Civil War broke out, resulting in the execution of King Charles I in 1649 and the eventual ascendancy of Oliver Cromwell. Cromwell then personally led the violent reconquest and subjugation of Ireland, effectively destroying any remaining Catholic landowning classes and further increasing British settlement, especially in the North. Continuing struggles over the British crown spilled onto Irish soil at the Battle of the Boyne in 1690 when the (Protestant) forces of William III defeated the (Catholic) forces of deposed James II. The victory solidified the Protestant ascendancy in British political life. In Ireland, the subsequent imposition of various Penal Laws institutionalized the political, economic, and religious discrimination of the Irish Catholic majority.

———

While there is a lengthy history of Irish resistance to British colonial rule, the failed Easter Uprising of 1916 marks the beginning of the successful Irish War of Independence, played out against the backdrop of the First World War. After winning a landslide victory in the general elections of 1918, the Irish republicans declared independence and, after three years of armed conflict, forced the British to the negotiating table. But their victory proved limited. In the six northern counties of Ireland, where Protestants outnumbered Catholics almost two-to-one, unionist parties had resoundingly won in the 1918 general election. These parties remained fiercely opposed to the possibility of Home Rule (establishing an Irish parliament in Dublin). Even before the Easter Uprising, roughly half a million unionists signed the 1912 Ulster Solemn League and Covenant (aka Ulster Covenant), pledging to resist Home Rule "by all means necessary." This division within Ireland was formalized by the 1920 Government Act of Ireland (known commonly as The Partition), in which the British government officially severed the six northern counties from the rest of the country, politically and geographically delineating Northern and Southern Ireland.

The Irish War of Independence ended in December 1921 with the Anglo-Irish Treaty, which established the self-ruled Irish Free State (eventually becoming the fully independent Irish Republic several years later). But the treaty allowed the six northern counties to remain part of the United Kingdom as the self-ruled Northern Ireland. The partition of the island was highly contentious in the Free State, directly contributing to the Irish Civil War

(1921–23). The war was fought between the newly created national army and anti-Treaty elements of the Irish Republican Army (IRA) who remained dedicated to a unified and independent Ireland. The government forces eventually proved victorious. Despite the Constitution of the Republic of Ireland claiming jurisdiction over the entire island, the six northeastern counties constituted a separate political entity known as Northern Ireland, which remains part of the United Kingdom to this day.

Brief History of Northern Ireland (1920–69)

By and large, religion served as a marker of political and social identity in Ireland. While the Gaelic language survived in the western region, most of the island's population was linguistically, as well as racially, homogeneous. One's religious affiliation became a shorthand marker to differentiate between descendants of British settlers and those of the socially and politically disenfranchised indigenous Gaelic Irish. After the partition, these distinctions largely disappeared in the predominantly Catholic South, in part because subsequent governments pursued policies aimed at social and economic egalitarianism (to varying degrees of success), but mostly because the minority Protestant landed gentry and their land holdings were targeted during the Irish War of Independence and the Civil War. The Protestant population within the Free State/Republic decreased from 10 percent (300,000) to 6 percent (180,000) in the twenty-five years following independence.[3] In contrast, these social and economic divisions remained highly relevant in Northern Ireland in the years that followed.

At the time of partition, Protestants outnumbered Catholics in Northern Ireland roughly two-to-one.[4] James Craig, the first prime minister of Northern Ireland, explicitly spoke of the country as a "Protestant state" ruled by a "Protestant parliament." He and his fellow political elites went to great lengths to ensure their positions of privilege, including gerrymandering and outright disenfranchisement and repression. For example, the 1922 Special Powers Act (in effect until Direct Rule was established in 1973) included, among other things, the banning of pro-republican meetings and parades, restrictions on flying the Irish flag, curfews, arrests without warrants, and internment without trial. Catholics, largely assumed to be sympathetic to the republican cause, faced profound systemic discrimination in most aspects of social, political, and economic life. Sectarian divisions permeated daily life, as children were often educated in different school systems and families tended to live apart in segregated neighborhoods.

Unlike the rest of the island, which largely experienced social and economic stagnation throughout the early twentieth century, Northern Ireland, and Belfast in particular, enjoyed significant economic growth and urbanization. This growth was largely due to industrialization, driven primarily by Belfast's shipbuilding industry (perhaps its most well-known product being the *Titanic*). However, employment at the shipyards was largely restricted to Protestants, undermining any sense of working-class solidarity. With the outbreak of the Second World War, the Republic of

Ireland declared itself "benevolently neutral," while feelings of patriotism strengthened loyalist sentiment in the North. As a major shipbuilding center, Belfast was important to the British war effort and, as such, was targeted by German bombers repeatedly. More than 900 civilians were killed and over half the homes in the city were damaged during the "Belfast Blitz" of early 1941.

Despite the bombing campaign, the war proved economically beneficial to Northern Ireland, producing a significant rise in employment. But given employment discrimination, the economic benefits were not felt equally across the population. Societal divisions deepened as Catholic communities faced growing economic and political exclusion, with Protestant communities often considering them disloyal enemies due to the Republic's declared neutrality. These years also saw the re-emergence of the Irish Republican Army (IRA) in the North, which sought assistance and weapons from Nazi Germany but was largely stifled by the harsh security measures on both sides of the border. A decade after the end of the war, the IRA initiated "Operation Harvest," a guerrilla-style border campaign lasting from 1956–62. It proved to be a resounding disaster both militarily and politically, failing to achieve a single victory or generate any degree of popular support. Yet, the IRA learned from this fiasco and shifted its tactics to engage with the growing civil rights movement emerging in the country.[5]

In 1967, the Northern Ireland Civil Rights Association (NICRA) was formed to protest widespread discrimination.[6] Though explicitly nonviolent, the movement was met with significant police brutality as well as violence from loyalist supporters, who feared the civil rights movement was a front for republicanism and communism. In general, these loyalists saw themselves under siege—while a privileged majority within Northern Ireland, they feared being a numerically insignificant minority if the republican goal of unification with the rest of Ireland ever succeeded. The violent response to the peaceful civil rights movement, combined with its failure to score any significant reforms, led to growing frustration among the republican communities. Feelings of victimization on both sides of the sectarian divide increasingly fueled extremism. By 1969, many on both sides of the debate no longer considered nonviolence a viable option, marking the beginning of the violent era known as the Troubles.

Life During the Troubles

Despite the common portrayal of the conflict in Northern Ireland as a religious struggle, it was, first and foremost, a political conflict. At its core, the Troubles were about the constitutional status of Northern Ireland, with unionists/loyalists wanting to remain in the UK and republicans/nationalists preferring to join the Republic of Ireland. The conflict also centered on whether all citizens should enjoy equal civil rights and liberties. However, the Troubles were often framed in terms of religious sectarianism (Catholic vs. Protestant) and ethno-nationalism (Irish vs. British), thus imbuing them with complex and problematic aspects of identity politics.

The violence characterizing the Troubles had many components across multiple fronts, involving the police, the army, and various paramilitary forces associated with the republican/nationalist and unionist/loyalist sides.[7] One major contributor to violence proved to be the police force itself, the Royal Ulster Constabulary (RUC). Since its creation in the 1920s, the RUC was known for its politicization and lack of professionalism.[8] Protestant loyalists comprised the group almost exclusively. Throughout its history, the RUC was supplemented by local Protestant paramilitary groups, the most infamous of which, the "B" Specials, functioned as a police auxiliary force whose primary purpose was the harassment of local Catholics. After being disbanded in 1969, the "B" Specials were replaced by the Ulster Defense Regiment (UDR).

The RUC proved to be unable to contend with the civil rights movement beyond violence and repression, leading to spiraling insecurity, especially in Belfast and Derry.[9] In a significant escalation, London deployed the British Army to Northern Ireland in 1969 to help maintain security. Originally seen as a neutral force, the army's heavy-handed actions, most notably in the shooting of twenty-six unarmed marchers in Derry's Bloody Sunday massacre on January 30, 1972, helped fuel the IRA's renewal. The prime minister of Northern Ireland at the time, Brian Faulkner, refused to transfer security matters to London, despite the mounting violence. In response, the British government suspended the Northern Ireland parliament and established Direct

Rule over the province (remaining in effect until the 1998 Good Friday Agreement). For Catholic communities, the British Army quickly became seen as a violent occupying force, protecting Protestant loyalist interests and harassing Catholic communities, thus adding a second layer of violence characterizing the Troubles.

Yet most of the violence was carried out by competing paramilitary organizations. With the crackdown on the nonviolent civil rights movement, the Irish Republican Army (IRA) initially focused on defending Catholic communities. A small splinter group, calling themselves the Provisional IRA (aka "Provos") and wanting to employ more offensive measures, emerged in December 1969. Originally a small group of extremists, the Provisional IRA became the dominant nationalist group by 1972, in contrast to the more Marxist-leaning "Official IRA" (aka "stickies"). Thus, after 1972, the label "IRA" usually refers to the Provisional IRA.

Feeling threatened by the civil rights movement, a group of unionists established the Ulster Volunteer Force (UVF) in 1965 and launched a campaign of bombings and random shootings against Catholic civilians the next year. The Ulster Defense Association (UDA; elements of which sometimes operated as the Ulster Freedom Fighters, UFF) formed in 1971 as an umbrella organization for a collection of loyalist forces. While smaller groups also existed, the three primary paramilitary groups were the IRA, UVF, and UDA.

In addition to competing campaigns of bombings and shootings, the early years of the Troubles involved the forced expulsion of families from integrated neighborhoods across Northern Ireland. In Belfast, this further heightened the sectarian-informed geography of the city. Starting in 1969, the authorities began erecting so-called "peace walls" across Belfast to separate sectarian communities from each other. Eventually entailing almost 100 walls, many of which still remain, the barriers stretched through the city for 30 kms (roughly 19 miles). The 1971 census indicated the demographic distribution within Northern Ireland had not greatly changed since the partition. Protestants still outnumbered Catholics in Northern Ireland, who remained roughly 30 percent of the population. Within Belfast, Protestants continued to outnumber Catholics by more than two-to-one. In the western region of the country, Catholics enjoyed a slight numeric advantage, including in the city of Derry.

While the Troubles brought violence to most corners of Northern Ireland, it was particularly acute in Belfast. On July 21, 1972, known as Bloody Friday, the IRA detonated over twenty bombs across the city (most within a half-hour period), resulting in ten dead and 130 injured. Reporter Kevin Myers of Radio Telefís Éireann (RTE) delivered memorable coverage of the event from the roof of RTE's Fanum House, one of the tallest buildings in the city at the time, as smoke rose from across the cityscape. As he noted later, "To witness what happened to Belfast that day from above was like seeing the hand of a terrible god, whose wrath was unquenchable and his means inexhaustible. The figures of ten dead and hundreds injured do not begin to capture the horror of that long-lost era."[10] The year 1972 proved to be the bloodiest of the conflict, with 480 killed (including 130 British soldiers) and almost 4,900 injured and maimed.

The yearslong deterioration of social and economic life in Northern Ireland was arguably a contributing factor to the rising violence. While Northern Ireland had proved far more economically developed than the rest of the island since the partition, the situation had changed by the 1970s. In 1973, both Ireland and the UK joined the European Economic Community (EEC; precursor to the European Union, EU). Yet, by then Northern Ireland had experienced years of significant economic stagnation, driven in large part by the relocation of much of the shipbuilding industry. Unemployment was high, with very few prospects in a dismal job market. In addition to declining industry, commercial activity had been markedly curbed by the bombing campaigns carried out by the various paramilitaries. For youths in Belfast, the future looked grim.

This desolation had its physical manifestation in the city centers of Belfast and Derry. The paramilitaries' bombing campaigns had turned those city centers into no-go zones. In Belfast, the central zone emptied as soon as the workday ended. The British army erected security barricades encircling the city center to keep bombers out. Everyone stayed in "their" segregated neighborhoods, which in turn were typically protected and policed by paramilitary forces. West Belfast was predominantly Catholic, while Protestants were the majority in East Belfast. Residents rarely intermingled. Protestant youths, for example, would rarely stray out of their Shankill neighborhoods, while Catholic youths hunkered down in the Falls, even though these two communities directly bordered each other. Within one's neighborhood, the youths encountered stultifying sectarianism, where conformity to the cause (whichever cause) was violently enforced.

At the same time, youths across Northern Ireland had very limited access to popular culture beyond regulated radio and television stations (with the significant exception of Radio Free Derry). One of the characteristics of life in Northern Ireland during this time was the lack of touring musical acts. Once renowned as a thriving destination for traveling bands and theater companies, by the 1970s Northern Ireland was a cultural wasteland. And while there were a few rare exceptions of visits by touring bands—such as Thin Lizzy and Horslips—the 1975 brutal murder of members of the Miami Showband by loyalist paramilitaries dressed as British soldiers underscored the dangers for musicians traveling to the North.

Meanwhile, across the Irish Sea, punk rock was beginning to send shockwaves across England.

Punk Comes to Belfast

The term "punk" entered common parlance in the late 1970s regarding the music scene emerging in New York City's Lower East Side, centered around the clubs CBGB and Max's Kansas City and characterized by such bands as the Ramones, Television, Blondie, Dictators, Heartbreakers, and others. But punk music and style gained international attention largely through the emergence of a scene centered in London. Informed partly by the New York scene, the London scene drew from antecedent subcultures of skinheads, mods, rude boys, glam rockers, as well as reggae, and rockabilly. Heavily conditioned by class politics and working-class culture, the London scene both reflected and mocked the disintegration of British society in the late 1970s. Rude and unconventional, punks viewed established social conventions as hypocritical obfuscations obscuring both the banality and brutality of everyday life. When discussing punk in his book *Lipstick Traces*, Greil Marcus observed: "as a sound, it seemed to make no sense at all, to make nothing, only to destroy, and this is why it was a new sound, and why it drew a line between itself and everything that came before it."[11]

On October 22, 1976, The Damned became the first UK punk band to release a single with "New Rose." The following month The Vibrators released their debut single "We Vibrate." But the Sex Pistols achieved national attention when, on November 26, 1976, they released "Anarchy in the UK." Actually, the national attention came a few days later when, on December 1, the band (accompanied by a few fans) were last-minute replacements on the popular TV show *Today* hosted by Bill Grundy. Provoked by a visibly drunk and lecherous Grundy, guitarist Steve Jones called the host a "dirty bastard," "dirty fucker," and "fucking rotter," igniting a national media storm.

Punk continued to pick up steam as a cultural force. April 1977 saw the release of The Clash's self-titled debut album to great acclaim. The next month, Petesy Burns—who later played in the punk band Stalag-17 and contributed to Belfast's Warzone Collective—listened to BBC Radio's weekly chart countdown in his Belfast childhood home. On that late May afternoon, the radio announcer explained he could not play a song rocketing up the charts because of broadcasting restrictions. The song was the Sex Pistols' second single. Released as a response to the Queen's Silver Jubilee commemorating Elizabeth II's twenty-five years on the throne, the song was called "God Save the Queen." But the BBC refused to play it on the radio and several publications simply inserted blank spaces when they reproduced the chart. Of course, Petesy wanted to hear the song. The next day, he headed downtown to his local record shop and bought the controversial single. For Petesy, this trip required a twenty-minute walk across hostile territory and across York Street, policed by the infamous Shankill Butchers. Upon arriving home, he put it on the turntable and his world suddenly shifted. The power of the music was overwhelming. "Oh fuck!" he thought. The singer Johnny Rotten pronounced the *"haitch"* in "H-bomb" like the working-class Irish kid he was, and Petesy felt an immediate kinship. Having been brought up in an Irish republican household, he related to the anger emanating from his speakers. It was, as he put it later, "one culture of resistance speaking to another."[12]

Similar transformations were taking place across Northern Ireland during late spring 1977. Youths who had never identified with popular music suddenly felt personal connections to punk. Kids who hadn't thought they could make their own music or art were now inspired to start their own bands and zines. In his own Belfast bedroom, a teenager named Brian Young had already discovered the Ramones. Previously steeped in a love of glam rock, Brian had formed a cover band a few months earlier. Energized by punk, he and his bandmates realized they could write their own songs. As a result, Rudi became Belfast's first punk band. Across town, the Cowan brothers—Martin, Colin, and Greg—heard the Sex Pistols, looked at each other and said, "That's just the greatest thing ever. We can do something like that!"[13] They didn't have instruments or the ability to play them yet, but they set out to form a band, eventually naming themselves the Outcasts after being turned away from five nightclubs in two weeks because of the way they looked.

Around this time, Henry Cluney, the guitarist for a teenage band called Highway Star specializing in hard rock cover songs, had also converted to punk. He eagerly shared this new music with his bandmates, but, to Henry's frustration, they were highly dismissive. The band's frontman, Jake Burns, listened to the music and shrugged it off as "rubbish."

2
From Highway Star to Stiff Little Fingers

In the Beginning: Forming Highway Star

John "Jake" Burns was born a decade before the outbreak of the Troubles, on February 21, 1958, in a working-class neighborhood off Oldpark Road in North Belfast. He was accepted into the Belfast Royal Academy but, fearing bullying by the local youths who regularly taunted the grammar school students, convinced his parents to send him to the nearby and less posh Belfast Boys Model. He was placed in the top 1A1 class.[1] Jake became interested in playing guitar after stumbling upon a broadcast on BBC Northern Ireland of the 1970 New Year's Eve farewell concert by Rory Gallagher's band Taste. Jake recalls, "I remember watching Rory Gallagher and thinking, 'That's what I want to do, that's what I want to be.'"[2]

The young Jake became obsessed with Gallagher, Led Zeppelin, and Black Sabbath, and badgered his parents to buy him a guitar. His dad worried the electric guitar would drive their electricity bills up, especially after he found out he would need to purchase an amplifier as well.[3] He eventually relented and took Jake down to the local Woolworths, where they found two models on display—one with two pickups and a cheaper single pickup model. Jake didn't want to be greedy, so he chose the cheaper guitar, later quipping: "I had no idea it would sound bloody awful."[4] Once in his possession, Jake slowly struggled to master the instrument. He later mused, "I've often joked that I had the guitar for a year and a half before I learnt how to tune it up and that's actually not that far from the truth."[5]

Eventually, Jake invited his friend Steve "Graymer" Graham to form a band. He then approached another 1A1 classmate who Jake thought "looked right" for the band.[6] Brian Faloon also hailed from a North Belfast working-class family. His father had originally been a plater's helper at Harland and Wolff shipbuilders but retrained as a welder after being made redundant. Brian recalls he wasn't originally sold on the idea of being in a band: "Originally I'd wanted to play keyboards, but I think Jake probably talked me out of that idea because he was primarily looking for a drummer."[7] Unfortunately, Brian had neither experience nor a drum kit: "I started out using biscuit tins, which I covered with taped-down plastic LP sleeves."[8]

Calling themselves Scruff, the band worked on learning covers, from T. Rex and Rolling Stones to heavier material by Led Zeppelin and Black Sabbath, as well as Irish bands such as Thin Lizzy, Taste, Skid Row, and Horslips. Looking for a place to practice, Jake asked the headmaster at Boys Model if they could use the school's central hall on weekends.

Surprisingly, the headmaster agreed, largely because he already spent most of his Sundays in the school marking papers. But they were soon forced to relocate to the physics laboratory because their loud rehearsals disturbed the services at the Ballysillian Road Presbyterian Church across the street.[9] They also solved Brian's problem of not having a kit by methodically pilfering the school's music room. Brian recalls, "We liberated a couple of drums from the school with the help of some friends and repainted them gold using car spray paint."[10] Around this time, Jake had his eye on a cool-looking, slightly older kid in the same grade but from the 1A2 (second highest) class.

Henry Cluney was relatively new to the school after his family, like so many others, fled their mixed neighborhood which had descended into a battleground between opposing republican and loyalist factions. Henry recalls,

> We lived in what was basically a Protestant area, but with a number of Catholic families. We lived about 300 yards from a police station. At night gunmen would be firing at the police station. We used to sleep underneath the beds with the wardrobe against the window, just in case. It just got so ridiculously dangerous that our mom and dad decided we had to get out of there.[11]

The family moved to the Shore Road and Henry attended Belfast Boys Model, where Jake marked him as "an interesting-looking character . . . with the longest hair in the school."[12]

Henry was a music fanatic, having traveled to the UK in 1975 to see the Rolling Stones perform live at the Knebworth rock festival—an unusual move for a Northern Irish teenager at the time—which increased his rock credibility among school peers. That same year, he received a guitar for Christmas, but not an amplifier. He remembers visiting Jake on Christmas Eve to borrow his. He often walked the four-mile round trip to Jake's house to get his new friend to tune the guitar and show him chords.[13] Henry learned quickly. Brian recalls, "Once he could play guitar Henry was unbelievable. He went away and learned literally hundreds of chords."[14]

Around this time, Steven Graham decided to leave Scruff to join another band rehearsing in the school. Henry soon joined Jake and Brian, working up cover songs and briefly calling themselves the BC Band (for Burns/Cluney). Looking for a bass player to round out the lineup, Jake asked an old friend, Gordon "Gordy" Blair, to join. They practiced regularly and worked up a decent set of covers, leaning heavily into the heavy rock bands of the time.

They were following the established showband template dominant in Northern Ireland at the time, working up popular covers with no original material.[15] As Jake noted, "Nobody would give you a gig writing your own material and apparently it never actually really dawned on us to write original material because who were we?"[16] A friend of the band booked them a show at the Helmsman Bar in Bangor, a coastal town northeast of Belfast. Reportedly playing for about a dozen people, including school friends and teachers they had convinced to attend, this first show was rather unremarkable, except for the last-minute decision to change the name of the band to Highway Star, taken from a

Deep Purple song off the 1972 *Machine Head* album. They continued practicing throughout 1976, amassing a two-hour set of covers from bands such as Dr. Feelgood, ZZ Top, Deep Purple, and Led Zeppelin, with an occasional pop song by the likes of the Bay City Rollers to "satisfy the younger crowd."[17] Jake would later self-deprecatingly observe, "we were not very good musicians. We were very limited . . . We never quite sounded enough like Lynyrd Skynyrd to get away with it."[18] But the fact that a teenage cover band regularly booked shows speaks highly of their musical abilities.

The Punk Conversion: Becoming Stiff Little Fingers

Yet a musical rift emerged within the band after Henry discovered punk. He arrived at the genre via an increasing obsession with pub rock, in particular the Essex band Eddie and The Hot Rods. Deeply enamored by their stripped-down sound and their "mach 10 delivery," he was primed for a punk rock conversion. Henry recalls, "I remember listening to John Peel on the radio, and he played 'Anarchy in the UK' by the Sex Pistols, the first Damned single ['New Rose'] and 'White Riot' by the Clash. And from then on that was me. I didn't want to hear anything else."[19]

The rest of the band remained unconvinced. Brian recalls, "Henry was certainly the first one of us to catch on to punk, he tried to educate us all from the very beginning; it took a while."[20] Jake begrudgingly agreed to incorporate a few Eddie and The Hot Rods songs into their set, but nothing by the Sex Pistols or Damned. Henry remained sullen, only becoming animated during their live shows when performing the faster songs. Otherwise, he sat indignantly on his amp for the classic rock tunes. "It's ridiculous saying it now," he recalls, "but we would be playing the songs, and I'd be yawning."[21] The management at Mooney's Bar was so irked by Henry's on-stage antipathy that they would only give Highway Star a regular slot if they kicked Henry out of the band. Personal narratives differ as to whether they actually sacked Henry for a time, but he continued playing with the band and advocating for the inclusion of punk songs in the set.[22]

For Jake, the conversion was a slow process. Henry bought most of his punk records from the two main stores in Belfast: Kyle Leitch's Caroline and Terri Hooley's Good Vibrations. He would bring them over to Jake's house in an attempt to convince his friend of their worth. He eventually brought over The Clash's debut album (released on April 8, 1977), but Jake remained unimpressed: "It sounded dead shoddy and so I didn't listen to the second side, I just left it." After being badgered by another friend about The Clash's version of Junior Murvin's "Police and Thieves," Jake returned to the album and concluded, "it was brilliant . . . I listened to it all again and realized what a superb album it was."[23] As he notes, "I played it and just sat with my chin round my ankles because I thought, 'This is just fantastic'—that's when it became life changing. That's when I realized, 'No, this is what I want to do.'"[24]

Once Jake got on board, Highway Star changed its musical direction, incorporating punk songs by The Clash, Damned, and Sex Pistols into their set. Continuing the showband cover formula, they were effectively a musical jukebox with a growing punk selection. Jake recalls, "Someone once memorably described us as a K-Tel punk band because we basically didn't have any material of our own at the time, so we just did what bands in Northern Ireland did, which you just became like a human jukebox."[25]

Adding the Sex Pistols' "God Save The Queen" to their set raised interesting challenges for the band. On the one hand, the song's anti-royalty sentiment might rile up loyalist members of the audience. But the bigger issue revolved around the lyric: "They made you a moron / a potential H-bomb." As Petesy Burns noted in the previous chapter, Johnny Rotten's pronunciation of the "*haitch*" had identified him as a working-class kid with Catholic Irish roots. Yet, like most Protestant kids in Belfast, that was not how the members of Highway Star pronounced it. Henry recalls the debate, "It was like, what do we sing? Do we sing '*haitch*' even though we don't say it that way? It became ridiculous—what do we do here? Because if we sing '*aitch*' are people gonna say, 'That's not the right words.'"[26] In the politically charged context of Northern Ireland, the question was not merely one of verisimilitude.

Around this time, bassist Gordon Blair departed the group. Again, there are differing opinions regarding why. Jake and Henry have both claimed Gordon left because he believed, in Jake's recollection, "fucking punk is rubbish."[27] This explanation seems suspect given Blair immediately joined Rudi, which can lay claim to being Belfast's first punk band. Rudi's Brian Young believes Gordon left Highway Star because he wanted to play original music. For his part, Brian Faloon suggested Blair was just unreliable and undependable (similar reasons were given when Blair was eventually booted from Rudi).[28]

After Blair's departure, the remaining three began constructing a punk-informed set with more covers by The Clash, Stranglers, Sex Pistols, Ramones, Damned, Dr. Feelgood, and Eddie and The Hot Rods. Brian remembers they strove to be as professional in their approach to punk as possible: "[Jake], Henry and I were determined to be the very best we could from the outset. I know the whole punk ethos was anyone can get up and do it, but we decided that we'd work at it, take it seriously and put the time in. Looking back I'd say we took the spirit of punk and imbued it with a professional attitude."[29] They were not the only showband of the era to convert to punk. The North Belfast Boogie Band, who also practiced in the same rehearsal spaces, reinvented themselves as the punk band Shock Treatment.

Looking for a new bassist, Jake was eventually connected to Alistair "Ali" McMordie, an accomplished bassist, by mutual friends. The four of them practiced together for the first time on June 4, 1977, at St. Peter's Church Hall. Ali was a student at Belfast Royal Academy, the school Jake resisted going to because it was too posh. He also hailed from North Belfast, specifically the Cliftonville area, which was experiencing increasing violence. A few months earlier, Ali's family had moved to avoid the fighting. As Ali recalls, "We were part of the general exodus from an increasingly dangerous and deteriorating drive-by area."[30] By the time he joined the band, Ali had already converted to punk: "The penny dropped when I heard the Ramones' first album, which we rushed down to Caroline Records and 'shoplifted' straight away. I remember Kyle [Leitch, co-owner] keeping a square eye on us to make sure that everything was paid for. It was important 'cos we had to get it straight away. It inspired us to stop listening to Deep Purple and Black Sabbath, tuck in the flares and cut the hair."[31] Before joining Highway Star, Ali had been playing in the local band Skull, which mutated into the Tearjerkers after his departure. Supposedly, Ali's first practice with Highway Star proved quite rough, as he played all the songs in a different key than Jake and Henry. This situation was resolved by their third practice, when Ali relearned all the songs in the key the others were playing.[32]

The new line-up decided they needed a more punk-sounding name. They originally adopted The Fast but dropped it after discovering the existence of an American band of the same name. Pressed to come up with a name for an upcoming gig, Jake recalls: "I grabbed the [Vibrators'] *Pure Mania* sleeve and looked at the titles and 'Stiff Little Fingers' was there so I said, 'Oh tell him we're called Stiff Little Fingers—we can always fucking change it after the first gig.'"[33]

They debuted on August 16, 1977—the day Elvis died—at the East Belfast pub Lambe's Lounge in the Ballyhackamore area. Brian Young, guitarist for Rudi, attended, curious to hear any band named after a Vibrators song. At the time, Brian assumed Rudi was the only punk band in Belfast. Arriving at the pub, he grew immediately suspicious upon seeing this new band was actually a rebranded Highway Star, whom he'd seen before and found unimpressive with "huge flares, long hair, cheesecloth shirts and Rory Gallagher guitar flailing."[34] But the band's reinvention impressed Brian: "They were about as punk as the Wombles, but I have to admit, musically you couldn't fault them. I'd even go so far as to say the performance was phenomenal."[35]

Yet, the venues for playing punk—even for Stiff's two-hour, covers-only set—were few. In fact, Lambe's Lounge banned punk shows the following week after The Outcasts debuted there. Before their raucous performance in front of a small but energetic audience convinced the management to prohibit punk gigs, The Outcasts made a significant discovery. They had set up the PA with everything running through a single amp and needed help sorting it out. Greg Cowan of The Outcasts recalls, "We didn't know anything about equipment or anything. Jake and Ali arrived and helped us. It was only then that we thought, 'God, there's another punk band?'"[36] At this point, given the social and physical divisions created by the Troubles, young punks in Belfast tended to remain isolated. If there was a rare show by one of the few local punk bands—at this point primarily Rudi, Outcasts, and SLF—most fans likely wouldn't know about it. And if they did, they might not be willing to risk crossing the violently policed social and geographical boundaries to get to the venue. But that was all about to change.

The Riot of Bedford Street

October 20, 1977, stands out as a historic date for Belfast punk. This was the date The Clash were scheduled to play in the city. Most touring bands had been avoiding playing in Northern Ireland for years. The 1975 brutal murder of members of the Miami Showband reinforced the risks for musicians traveling to the North. The Clash had booked a gig at the Ulster Hall, but the show was cancelled hours before doors opened. It still remains unclear why, possibly due to paramilitary threats, failure to acquire insurance, or nervous promoters. By that point, a large crowd of punks had already gathered in front of the venue. The police arrived, tensions escalated, punks threw rocks, and the "Riot of Bedford Street" entered local lore.[37] The members of Stiff Little Fingers were there, with Ali receiving blows from police truncheons while others made their way to the nearby Europa Hotel to talk with members of The Clash through a chain link fence. The band promised to return to Belfast, which they did several months later.

The scale of the rioting wasn't significant. As Paul Burgess, who would go on to drum for the band Ruefrex (originally Roofwrecks), recalls, "Everybody talks about the riot, but in terms of Belfast riots, it was about two out of ten. There was a bit of to-ing and fro-ing with the cops. People were working themselves into a bit of a frenzy."[38] The significance of the event was that most of the fans had assumed they were the only punks in the city. This sense of isolation had been exacerbated by the fact that everyone largely kept to their own neighborhoods, policed (literally and figuratively) by sectarianism. But here were dozens of Catholic and Protestant kids realizing they had punk in common. Jake recalls, "There was a lot of people milling around and causing a disturbance outside the Ulster Hall and what amazed me was not the fact that they were causing a disturbance—because, after all, it was Belfast—but the number of people that was there . . . I suddenly realized that it wasn't just the four of us, that there were a lot of people out there who actually were listening to this sort of stuff."[39] Punks and punk bands already existed in Belfast, but the Riot of Bedford Street brought disparate individuals together, both cementing and expanding the Belfast scene in a matter of hours. As Martin McLoone, a professor of media studies, wrote about the evening, "The disappointed Belfast punks who turned up for the gig in a sense found each other . . . On that night, in other words, the individual punks of Belfast coalesced into 'a scene' and many of the bands that would emerge in the next few months could trace their genesis back to these events."[40]

But just as the Belfast scene was coalescing, the few accessible venues started closing their doors to punk shows. Rudi, who had been playing for almost a year, suddenly found themselves unwelcome at venues that had previously been happy to have them. Likewise, Stiff Little Fingers were being turned away from venues that had booked Highway Star months earlier. Fortunately, Rudi had been employing a DIY approach to booking for some time: hiring out function rooms at hotels on the outskirts of the city, under the guise of throwing a private party, and then selling "invitations" to guests when they arrived. Thus, DIY punk gigs were held in places such as the Glenmachan Stables (literally an old stabling ground) and Girton Lodge in East Belfast. Rudi invited other emerging Belfast punk bands to join their gigs, and others, such as The Outcasts and Stiff Little Fingers, adopted a DIY approach to booking by necessity.[41]

One of the few venues in Belfast willing to book punk shows was the Pound Music Club on Townhall Street. Kyle

Leitch, a shop assistant at Caroline Music, approached the owners. "I told him something along the lines of, 'You've got nothing to lose by letting these bands play, the weekday evenings are always dead.'"[42] The venue was dark and dingy with a low ceiling and stone walls and floors. As for its name, it historically served as a literal pound for the holding of livestock for the Belfast market. But it provided an important foothold for the growing punk scene.

Two Journalists Walk into a Bar . . .

Employing a similar DIY approach to self-promotion, Jake began sending letters out to the local press. As he recalls, "I basically wrote these really snotty, cheeky letters . . . it was punk rock, it was what you did, you know, you had no respect for anybody. I seem to recall one of the lines I wrote was, 'We're the best thing that's happened to music since Van Morrison fucked off.'"[43] One of the people he targeted was Colin McClelland of the *Belfast Sunday News*. McClelland grew up in North Belfast, having attended the Belfast Royal Academy, and wrote two regular columns: "Follow Me Around," in which he shared thoughts and opinions, and "Colin McClelland's Nightlife," about various social events he attended. They struck up an occasional correspondence and, in the August 21, 1977, edition of the paper, McClelland wrote: "I have received several letters from a strange group of people who call themselves Stiff Little Fingers. To get them off my back, I have decided to publish the last of their missives in full." He then proceeded to reproduce Jake's letter in its entirety, in which Jake introduced the band and appealed for gigs: "We are looking for lots of lovely work that will bring us lots of lovely money so we can afford to pay for real advertising."[44]

McClelland was friends with English journalist Gordon Ogilvie of the *Daily Express*. As Colin recalls,

> One evening Gordon and I got to talking about the emergence of punk and by then we both agreed that The Clash were probably the most exciting thing that had happened to music since Elvis in the Fifties. I remember this led Gordon to suggest that surely as the music of disaffected and angry youth, the most valid punk bands should be in Northern Ireland. At that point I mentioned that the only local punk band that I'd heard of, or had any contact with, was this group called Stiff Little Fingers, who I intended to go see at the Glenmachan [Stables].[45]

Ogilvie joined McClelland to see the band's gig on Monday, November 14, 1977. Gordon recalls, "I remember being immediately impressed with how tight they were and saying to Colin, 'If this is a garage band then they must have been a long time in the garage rehearsing.' They came across as pretty professional."[46] Indeed, that professionalism set them apart from many of the other punk bands emerging at the time, such as the ramshackle (and occasionally violent) Outcasts. But they also stood out for being a punk rock jukebox band, playing nothing but covers, which the journalists noted.

Immediately after the show, the two journalists approached the Stiffs and offered to help the band out in any way they could. The next week, they met up with Jake at the Shaftesbury Inn pub on Atrium Road and offered to help with publicity. Colin recalls that "Jake pushed for more and stated that the band was looking for management . . . Subsequently we became, what I call, reluctant managers."[47] At the Shaftesbury Inn meeting, Gordon asked Jake if the band had written any original material. By that time, Jake had written two songs, "State of Emergency" and "Breakout," but because the band hadn't played either at the Glenmachan Stables show, the journalists assumed the band only played covers. Gordon pushed Jake, asking if he had written any songs about Belfast and the Troubles, especially by using an everyday phrase. Jake didn't understand Gordon's meaning: "I still couldn't see what he was talking about. I was thinking about everyday phrases that we have in Belfast like the standard greeting, which is 'What about ye?' and I thought, 'No, that's not very useful, what's he talking about?'" Eventually Gordon pulled a sheet of paper out of his pocket, offering it to Jake. "He handed it to me and I read it—I could literally feel the fucking pub spin and I thought 'This is fantastic. I can use this.'"[48]

The sheet contained the complete lyrics to a song Ogilvie had written called "Suspect Device."

3
The Singles
"Suspect Device" and
"Alternative Ulster"

After Gordon handed Jake the lyrics to "Suspect Device," he went home and wrote the music for the song and composed another song, "Wasted Life," in a single night. When the two journalists stopped by the rehearsal space the next week, the band played both songs in what would be close to their final form. Everything with the band started changing.

"Suspect Device"

When Gordon first saw the Stiffs at the Glenmachan Stables a few weeks earlier, he had been so impressed that he went home and wrote the entire lyrics to "Suspect Device" in one go. As he recalled,

> it was a phrase, which seemed to feature in every news bulletin at the time . . . I remember sitting up very late one night and pouring everything I thought about the

Troubles in particular and adolescence in general into it. It is about the most intensively creative I have ever been in my life and I'm still proud to rediscover, from time to time, how well I managed to encapsulate so much of what I thought into one short lyric. I'm not saying it is Shakespeare or Dylan or even Brian Wilson, but it does the job and obviously has struck a chord with a few people.[1]

The phrase "suspect device" has a double meaning within the song. On the one hand, it refers to incendiary devices that the paramilitary forces, particularly the IRA, had begun employing in their bombing campaigns. 1972 had proven to be the deadliest year of the Troubles, with more than 12,000 shooting and bombing attacks across Northern Ireland and a death toll of 480. Belfast and Derry bore the brunt of the violence. The authorities, now supported by the British Army, had initiated a brutal but largely effective crackdown. In response, the IRA shifted its tactics away from an "insurgency" to a "terrorist" approach.[2] By 1977, the number of attacks had been reduced to around 2,800, but their nature had become more random as the use of homemade bombs increased. IRA bombs tended to utilize gelignite or commercial fertilizers, smuggled across the border from the Republic.[3] While car and mail bombs were significant features of the campaign, many of the incendiary devices were also placed in parcels and left in pubs or other public spaces. Sometimes a coded call would be made to alert authorities to the bomb's location, but other times not.

Thus, citizens of Belfast and across Northern Ireland grew accustomed to keeping an eye out for "suspect devices."

The other meaning of the term within Ogilvie's lyrics referenced the Belfast punks' resistance to their parents' stifling sectarianism. Having witnessed how Belfast punks were rejecting the violent binary informing life in Northern Ireland, Gordon praised the youthful rebellion challenging the divided society. The punk scene emerging in Belfast was creating a safe, non-sectarian space for Northern Irish youths (discussed further in Chapter 5), but Gordon envisioned something greater: punks as an active anti-sectarian force. In his vision, punks themselves became "suspect devices." As Gordon notes, "I've always had a great respect for teenage rebellion. The lyrics are essentially saying, don't be a kid caught up in this. Don't perpetuate it. Find some way to stop it happening."[4]

The song opens with an aggressive guitar line, one that Jake admits to lifting directly from "Space Station #5" by the California rock band Montrose (featuring a young Sammy Hagar on lead vocals).[5] Then Jake snarls, "Inflammable material, planted in my head / It's a suspect device that's left two thousand dead." As Stuart Baillie has observed, "At the time of the meeting with Gordon and Colin, the death toll from the conflict was 1,978. By the time the song had been recorded and released, the toll was 2,012."[6] As Jake's vocals accentuate the word "dead," the rest of the band kicks in. Jake continues, framing the situation in stark us-vs.-them terms. Though "they" remain nameless throughout, the song is an open indictment against all the perpetrators of the conflict.

The "us" are the young, innocent victims who want nothing to do with the armed struggle.

Jake, singing Ogilvie's words, urges the listener not to believe the "bastards" and avoid getting "bitten twice." He tells the listener to question everything they are told, seize control, and fix the situation. This call for self-empowerment and resistance is articulated in the chorus as he calls on the listeners to be their own "suspect device." In the last verse, his/Gordon's call for rebellion reaches its apex as Jake proclaims: "I'm a suspect device the Army can't defuse / You're a suspect device they know they can't refuse." As the music reaches its crescendo, Jake barks out one of the best closing lines in the history of rock 'n' roll: "We're gonna blow up in their face!"

When the Sex Pistols slagged off the monarchy, the response amounted to little more than some clutched pearls and maybe a bit of street harassment. At worst, their single was banned by the BBC and whited-out on the record charts. To be clear, the Stiff Little Fingers were doing far more than criticizing the political authorities. They were calling out the armed paramilitary forces responsible for hundreds of murders. As such, these were stunningly provocative lyrics. And the paramilitaries took notice.

Impressed by what Jake had done with his lyrics, Gordon encouraged the band to record a demo of the song so it could be shopped around to record companies. On Saturday, February 4, 1978, Colin booked the band into the Downtown Radio eight-track studio in Newtownards, which the radio station used to record advertising jingles. Gordon banned alcohol from the studio to ensure the young band members completed the recording in the few available hours. Engineer

Stephen "Rastus" Nelson set up the mics in front of the amps and had the band run through both "Suspect Device" and "Wasted Life" as if they were playing live. Unfortunately, Jake was suffering from a cold at the time, so he had to return a few evenings later to record the vocals.[7]

The recording was meant to be a demo to shop around to prospective record labels. But pressing plants wouldn't press anything less than 500 records. The band was unsure how to proceed, so Gordon offered to cover the £500 cost for the recording and pressing of a single, with the intention of distributing the extra copies to local record stores. Jake recalls, "I had no idea at all that you could make your own. I thought you had to be signed to fucking EMI or something before you could make a record. Again, that whole side of the punk thing completely passed me by because people were doing it all the bloody time, but not in Belfast they weren't."[8]

Colin and Gordon set up a management company and record label under the name Rigid Digits (a pun on the band's name supplied by a school friend of Ali's). Their newly created label ordered 500 copies of "Suspect Device" to be pressed by Cardel, a Dublin-based pressing plant, with "Wasted Life" on the B-side. Though the lyrics to the A-side were written by Ogilvie and the music by Burns, the song was credited to "Fingers/Ogilvie," which became the standard practice for all songs co-written by the two. Explaining why he included the rest of the band, Jake noted: "We decided to put Fingers on everything to denote band democracy and avoid individuals wanting three songs on every album etc. Gordon wasn't in the band but did contribute lyrics so always had the separate credit."[9] The band and the two journalists-turned-managers agreed to split all income six ways.

Released on St. Patrick's Day (17 March) 1978, Gordon and Colin utilized their media contacts to secure a full-page feature dedicated to the record's release in the Irish edition of the *Daily Mirror*. The single received favorable reviews in the UK, most of which played upon the band's Belfast roots. In *Melody Maker* (March 25, 1978), Ian Birch wrote: "Belfast girds it fatigues; enter a new-wave quartet hellbent on bringing their doorstep to your cosy stereo. Aggressive, abusive and forthright in Clash/Pistols tradition with all the dubious implications that such a style suggests."[10] In a March 1978 piece in the influential *New Musical Express* entitled "It's a Dog's Life in Today's Belfast," Jake played up the band's authenticity as a street-tough Belfast band while criticizing The Clash and Sex Pistols for their "comparatively cushy" standpoints, stating: "they can't judge real repression until they come here."[11] But back home in Belfast, the response was more muted, with Gavin Martin of *Alternative Ulster* observing: "Stiff's debut is moderate but very overrated, there's much better songs in their repertoire."[12]

The front cover of the single featured a photo of a collection of IRA incendiary devices seized by the army over the course of the previous year, which Gordon had "obtained" from the *Daily Express*'s archives.[13] The back cover contained a black-and-white photo of the band taken on the "peace line" wasteland between the Catholic Falls and Protestant Shankill roads. But to save money, it was decided the band would print and construct the sleeves themselves, which entailed a good bit of cutting, folding, gluing, and pressing.

In what has become an infamous bit of band lore, Gordon sent out a handful of cassette versions of the single to UK record labels, news agencies, and radio stations. The cover of the cassette featured a black-and-white image of a single incendiary device (as opposed to the collection used on the vinyl sleeve). Included was a press release stating: "This is one terrorist incendiary cassette that will not go off in your face. But we reckon the music inside may still blow you [away]." Admittedly a provocative publicity stunt, given the IRA's active bombing campaign at the time (often using time-delayed cassette incendiary devices left in commercial shops and businesses), the imagery played upon the band's Belfast roots. At the time, Jake observed: "It gets across what we're about. And it might get us noticed. That's exactly what we want to achieve."[14] As Henry recalls, "I think it was Gordon's idea, putting them in the cassette with the wiring printed and things on it, obviously it's a publicity stunt. But coming from Belfast at the time we thought, 'It's either gonna get you noticed or it's gonna get you into trouble.' So, we thought, 'Well, what have we got to lose?' Looking back on it now, okay, it's a bit corny, but it was like, you gotta use what you've got that you can use. And that's what we did."[15]

A rumor quickly emerged—likely started by the band or its management—that one of the record companies, fearing a real bomb, threw the cassette into a bucket of water. Gordon later distanced himself from the rumor: "I've heard stories this caused panic in EMI or wherever, and people dropped them into buckets of water and stuff, but that has to be complete and utter bollocks. Because, quite clearly, it was a black and white photo. It was clearly packaging."[16] But in an interview more than two decades later, Jake was still recycling the story, stating, "We sent it off to record companies to try and get a deal and at least one phoned us back and said, 'Can you send us another copy? We've thrown that one in a bucket of water!' They saw the Belfast postmark, opened it up, saw this, panicked and put it in a bucket of water."[17] As enduring as it is, the story is certainly not true. But the incident illustrates the determination of the band and management to do what they could to get noticed.

Fortunately for the band, they did get noticed by influential radio DJ John Peel. He began playing the song repeatedly on his weeknight BBC show *Top Gear*, which ran from 10 p.m. to midnight. For several weeks running, Peel played it almost every night. This exposure proved to be the breakthrough the band needed. Speaking to *Melody Maker* later that year, Jake observed: "All of a sudden we were from nowhere to the biggest name in Northern Ireland."[18] Geoff Travis, the owner of Rough Trade, an independent and influential record store in London, was so taken by the song that he tracked down the band to buy as many copies as he could. Up to that point, the single was only available outside Northern Ireland at Scotia, an Edinburgh record store Gordon had convinced to carry fifty copies, shipping them over in a bakery supplies van. Seeing a need, Travis ordered extra copies to distribute to other record stores in England, establishing Rough Trade as a distribution company. Given the interest from Scotia and Rough Trade, as well as the important Belfast stores Caroline and Good Vibrations, Rigid Digits quickly sold out of the original 500 copies. Colin ordered another 1,500 pressed, but these too moved quickly, driven largely by Peel's continuous promotion of the single. Sales soon outpaced the band's DIY record sleeve production. An oft-repeated story has the band and friends gluing the sleeves together by hand while listening to the Peel show. When Peel played "Suspect Device" yet again, everyone began yelling at the radio. Jake recalls, "We were going, 'Fuck off, stop playing it, stop playing the fucking record' because we couldn't keep up with the fucking demand, which is a fantastic position to be in but we were genuinely saying, 'Stop doing it, I don't want to hear it anymore.'"[19] As soon as Rigid Digits began making a profit from the release, they started printing the sleeves commercially.

Ultimately, Rigid Digits went through seven pressings of the single, selling between 20–25,000 copies. Exactly one year after its original release, Rough Trade would re-release the single for them. That version would sell over 25,000 more copies.[20]

The success of "Suspect Device" also increased media attention on the growing Belfast punk scene. Thanks to their aggressive management team, the band quickly became the face of that scene, at least in the media. Ulster TV sent a crew to film performances by SLF and Victim at the Pound, broadcasting a half-hour show on March 6, 1978 entitled "It Makes You Want to Spit."[21] By this point, numerous other bands were emerging to join the original Belfast punk pioneers. As Jake observed, "Six months after we first played, there were hundreds of the buggers, but, when we first started, it was just the three of us and there was a definite rivalry between all three bands. In the case of Rudi and ourselves, it became quite a friendly rivalry but The Outcasts always kept themselves apart from that."[22] Greg Cowan from The Outcasts recalls,

> Bands are very jealous creatures, incredibly jealous, especially us. We watched every other band become more successful than us. It was violent at times. You're doing what you can to spoil their fun. I was incredibly jealousy of Stiff Little Fingers, incredibly jealous of the other teams. Now I really like the guys, but still incredibly jealous of them, let's be honest.[23]

The intrinsic rivalry within the Belfast scene, coupled with the outsized media attention on Stiff Little Fingers, led to increased criticism of the band from some corners—criticism that would grow over time. Many of the other punk bands looked upon SLF with a degree of suspicion, questioning their dedication to the punk cause. It is worth noting that at this time the Stiffs were still essentially a cover band. For the show recorded by UTV, of the thirty-four songs the band played, only five were original and twenty-nine were covers. Many in the Belfast scene still considered them little more than a long-haired, hard rock cover band that were jumping on the punk bandwagon.

Suspicion also hovered around the band due to the presence of the two journalists taking on the band's management role. When it became known that Ogilvie was providing lyrics and ideas for songs, suspicion and resentment greatly increased. Many understandably questioned the validity of an English journalist's take on life in Belfast.

Moreover, many in the scene accused the band of exploiting the Troubles for their own gain. The PR stunt featuring the incendiary cassette cover rubbed many within the Belfast scene the wrong way. Yet, the band's management leaned into their exoticized presentation of the band and their Belfast environs. The UK media coverage of the band, clearly shaped by Colin and Gordon's PR material, employed what many back home regarded as tired and misinformed tropes and clichés, often celebrating the band for rising above "war-torn bloody Belfast" to make music for "kids across the barricades."[24]

In what may be the most egregious marketing move of their career, Gordon began claiming the band was "mixed"— made up of two Catholics and two Protestants. Anyone with a passing familiarity with the band and their background would recognize this as a complete lie. All four were clearly from Protestant neighborhoods in North Belfast and had attended Protestant schools. Everyone in the Belfast punk scene knew this and was gobsmacked by the claim.[25] Even some of the band members were uncomfortable with this deception. As Brian Faloon recalls, "When Gordon pushed the idea that the band was compromised of two Protestants and two Catholics, I remember we weren't very pleased at all. In particular, I think, Henry was very against it. Although we were all brought up as non-sectarian, we were four Protestant guys from north Belfast. I was also very aware that making incorrect claims like that could have a very good chance of coming back at us."[26] Despite their misgivings, all four of the band members became complicit in the deception, not offering to correct the record. Amazingly, this is a lie that still continues today. As of 2025, the claim can still be found on their Wikipedia page. When asked about it in a 2003 interview, Jake continued fostering this false claim, neglecting to set the record straight.[27]

Promoting the band as "mixed" and playing up the cartoonish clichés of the Northern Ireland conflict was a calculated move by Gordon and Colin to break through the noise of the music industry. While other Northern Irish punk bands at the time—such as Rudi, The Outcasts, and The Undertones in Derry—intentionally chose not to play upon the Troubles, the Stiff Little Fingers exploited the connection as fully as possible to create a distinctive identity (their brand, if you will) that would set them apart from other punk and new wave bands. Brian Young of Rudi recalls, "Tellingly, most NI bands steered clear of trite political sloganeering, wary of being seen as cashing in on the situation here. Growing up in Northern Ireland many folks were sick to death of party politics and unwilling to be pigeonholed along traditional lines, which would have been divisive and maybe dangerous too!"[28] In hindsight, the managers were quite Machiavellian in their approach, and the band proved more than willing to go along. Speaking to *NME* soon after the release of "Suspect Device," Jake stated, "Obviously we want our music to be heard by as many people as possible, and we're not in this business for any other reason. We want to be famous, the same as everybody else."[29] A major label would soon come courting, but first, the band needed to write more original material.

"Alternative Ulster"

Within the Belfast scene, one of the earliest and most popular fanzines was *Alternative Ulster*. Co-edited by Gavin Martin and Dave McCullough (joined later by Roger Pearson), the zine's first issue (#7; they employed an unorthodox approach to numbering issues) had a print run of only fifty copies and was released in September 1977. *Alternative Ulster* provided the best coverage of punk in Northern Ireland and quickly grew in popularity, size, and coverage (a young Stephen Morrissey would regularly write from Manchester). The zine approached Rudi about releasing their song "Big Time" on a flexidisc to be included in a future issue, but the band opted to press the single on vinyl with Terri Hooley's Good Vibrations label instead. Undeterred, the editors then approached Stiff Little Fingers about having "Suspect Device" released as a flexi. The band declined because they wanted the song on their own Rigid Digits label. But Jake offered to write a new song just for them, utilizing the title of the zine. There is some disagreement over what happened next. Gavin Martin has claimed the zine editors decided it wasn't cost effective.[30] But Jake maintains that when the band played the song for Martin, he hated it.[31] Either way, the zine passed on the flexidisc idea, and the band had a new original song.

On March 30, 1978, the band opened for pub rockers Eddie and The Hot Rods at the Ulster Hall in Belfast. The Stiffs so impressed Ed Hollis, the Hot Rods' manager,[32] he told them he wanted to bring them to England to record a demo for Island Records, the label for Eddie and The Hot Rods. The band dismissed his offer as drunken ramblings. But, true to his word, Hollis convinced the record label to check out the Stiffs. Gordon soon received a call from Island Records asking him to organize a showcase in Belfast so their reps could check out the band live. The hastily organized performance at Belfast's Regency Hotel convinced the label's reps, and Island flew the band to London for a two-day recording stint. They used the label's small basement studio in St Peter's Square, Chiswick from May 20–21, 1978. With Ed Hollis producing, the Stiffs quickly knocked out demo versions of "Alternative Ulster" and "78 RPM."

A week later, the Island reps called and offered the band a £35,000 advance with plans to fly them back to London for a public contract signing. The label encouraged the band to quit their jobs, which Jake (an accountant's clerk at Mackie International) and Brian (a telex operator at F. G. Wilson Engineering) both did. Given the staggeringly high levels of unemployment in Northern Ireland at the time, quitting their jobs had serious implications.[33] Ali was still technically a student and Henry was unemployed and on the dole. Two days before their departure, Island called and told the band they were reneging on the promised deal. By all accounts, Chris Blackwell, the Island Records boss who had been on vacation during the earlier negotiations, killed the deal when he returned and heard the demos.

The news devastated the band. They briefly considered throwing in the towel. But the debacle eventually increased the determination of at least three quarters of the band. Upon hearing about the Island Records debacle from Gordon, Geoff Travis of Rough Trade offered to put out their next single. After getting into the distribution business with "Suspect Device," the record store had released three singles under the Rough Trade label. This would be their fourth.

There were two problems. First, everyone hated the Ed Hollis mix. Jake claimed that "Ed wanted to take all the edge and rawness off the band."[34] Henry agrees: "the production was a bit clean for Stiff Little Fingers in that it was less punky or rocky sounding. It had more of a pop feel."[35] The second and seemingly more serious problem was that Island remained in possession of the master recordings. The band disagrees about how they acquired the tapes. Jake and Ali claim the band obtained the tapes through trickery and deceit.[36] But Henry and Gordon maintain it was a straightforward affair. Gordon has stated, "As I recall there was no skullduggery or subterfuge. I collected the tapes. They knew I was coming and I signed a formal release letter confirming they belonged to us."[37] Regardless, once they were in the band's possession, Rough Trade's Geoff Travis (who had no previous experience in a recording studio) worked with record store colleague Steve Montgomery to remix the songs, using Doug Bennett as the engineer. To the band's delight, they salvaged what were otherwise regarded as flaccid demos. Jake would go on to tell *Hot Press* in 1980: "[Doug Bennett] brought out what was really good with it and put a bit of life into it. The difference is fucking phenomenal."[38]

Rough Trade released the single on October 17, 1978, as the band wrapped up a UK tour opening for the Tom Robinson Band.[39] The sleeve featured an intentionally provocative photograph of a British soldier crouching behind a battered concrete pillar, his rifle poking around the corner. A young boy in a parka jacket is perched atop the pillar, looking down at the soldier, laughing, and unafraid. Most Belfast residents would recognize the location: a military base on Springfield Road, directly across the road from the Henry Taggart Memorial Hall and one of the sites of the

Ballymurphy killings of 1971. A friend of Gordon's, *Daily Express* staff photographer Milton Haworth, had taken the photo in 1974. As Haworth recalled: "The picture was taken when I got wind of shots being fired at an army patrol. I raced to the area and stationed myself behind a wall, parallel with a couple of soldiers as the army searched my area. As I focused on one of the squaddies, up popped this cheeky young scamp and started mugging for the camera. It isn't a montage. It's exactly as shot."[40] It is a powerful image. Jake stated, "We put a soldier with a kid pissing himself laughing on the cover [because it] seemed to sum the whole bloody thing up."[41]

If it is true that Gavin Martin, co-producer of the *Alternative Ulster* zine and future editor for the *NME*, dismissed the song as "shite" upon hearing it, one should well question his musical judgment. Writing about the song years later, Stuart Bailie (a frequent critic of the band) observed, "If these words were to hit you at the right moment they could be life-changing."[42] It is not a stretch to claim "Alternative Ulster" is the best song Stiff Little Fingers ever wrote. Some, myself included, are willing to argue that it ranks as one of the greatest punk songs ever, and probably the most important song to ever come out of Northern Ireland. It is no wonder the song has since been repeatedly referred to as the country's unofficial national anthem.

Jake wrote the song with Gordon offering only one minor lyrical suggestion.[43] Supposedly, Jake was inspired musically by Bob Marley's "No Woman No Cry," which has a similar chord progression. Interestingly, The Edge would later admit U2's "With or Without You" was written by playing "Alternative Ulster" very slowly, also employing the same D/A/Bm/G chord progression. While the opening guitar riff of "Alternative Ulster" is instantly recognizable, the song's power comes from its lyrics and vocal delivery. With regard to the latter, Bailie has observed, "Jake Burns sang the lyrics in a hurry, like a guy in a phone box with no spare change."[44] This lends the song a sense of urgency, as Jake demands your attention.

Jake has repeatedly claimed the lyrics to "Alternative Ulster" have been misconstrued. Speaking to *Melody Maker* in 1980, Jake stated the song was just "about being bored out of your skull in Belfast."[45] Decades later, in a 2003 interview with the *Guardian*, Jake continued to downplay the political implications of the song: "It was a song written in the classic punk mode about having nothing to do, because that was the over-riding reality of life in Belfast for a teenager in the mid-Seventies. Not fear of riots, or bombs, or whatever. It was the sheer tedium of having nowhere to go and nothing to do when you got there."[46] In an interview with Alan Parker the same year, Jake argued, "Lots of people made lots of claims on its behalf and, in fact, it really is the classic punk rock I-am-bored-and-I-have-got-nothing-to-do song. That's all it's about and yet people see this as a big political statement about life in Northern Ireland. And, by its nature, any comment on life in Northern Ireland was bound to be political and basically all it was was, 'I am fed up, I've got nothing to do.'"[47]

With all due respect to Jake Burns, this self-deprecating argument regarding the apolitical nature of the lyrics is absolute bollocks. Admittedly, the first verse of the song articulates a clear sense of boredom. The first line bemoans the fact that there is nothing to do in Belfast, lamenting the decrepit nature of The Pound. The reference, of course, is not the British currency but the low-ceilinged venue in the center of Belfast that was once literally a pound for holding livestock. Jake continues by namechecking the Trident in Bangor, another punk-friendly pub (and not the nuclear-powered submarine of the same name). The year before, Rudi convinced the landlord of the Trident to allow them and other punk bands to play there. Unfortunately, Bangor is a coastal town about 13 miles northeast of Belfast. If Belfast punks missed the last bus and train back to the city, it was a long walk home.

So far, it does sound like a classic nothing-to-do punk song. As the chorus kicks in, Jake seems to be urging the listener to either pick up a copy of the *Alternative Ulster* zine or take matters into their own hands: "What we need is an alternative Ulster/ Grab it and change it, it's yours." Maybe it is just a catchy promo piece for the zine or a frustrated appeal for more to do on a Saturday night. But then the chorus takes on a decidedly different tone when Jake urges the listener to be an "an anti-security force." If this were just a song about being bored, there would be no need for that entreat. The chorus then concludes with what is reportedly Gordon's only contribution to the song—and what a contribution it is, with its explicit call for engagement and the envisioning of a better tomorrow by altering "your native Ulster," by altering "your native land."

By the second verse, one can completely dispense with Jake's claims that the song was merely about the tedium of life in Belfast. It opens with a powerful command: "Take a look where you're livin'." It's a challenge, a provocation, a demand that the listener engage in greater self-awareness. Then, instead of singing about run-down old punk venues, Jake delivers what might be the most biting description of life within the context of the Troubles: "You got the Army on the street and the RUC dog of repression is barking at your feet/ Is this the kind of place you wanna live? Is this where you wanna be?" Obviously, the answer is decidedly no.

On the heels of that powerful verse, the chorus now takes on even greater weight. It represents a call for envisioning a better life, one beyond the indiscriminate violence of the hateful sectarianism permeating every aspect of life in Northern Ireland. Jake tells the listener we can do better. We have to. Not only can we imagine an alternative future, we must do everything we can to bring that vision to reality.

With the third verse, Jake employs a familiar us-vs.-them attitude, underscoring the need for resistance and personal empowerment: "And they say they're a part of you / And that's not true, you know / They say they've got control of you / And that's a lie, you know / They say you will never be free." It's not clear if he is speaking about parents, political authorities, paramilitary forces, or all of the above, but his anger is visceral and moving. Jake may have started out intending to write a song about being bored in Belfast, but he crafted something much more monumental in the process.

In under three minutes, the Stiff Little Fingers sowed powerful seeds of resistance with nothing but a microphone, bass, guitars, and drums. With "Alternative Ulster" they constructed an enduring and damning document about the Troubles, while simultaneously conjuring and celebrating youthful resistance. Building upon the name of the zine, it's a rejection of the stultifying present and an imagining of a promising future. Two simple words became both an acute idea and a call for radical action. Moreover, these two minutes and forty-four seconds tell you everything you need to know about the ways in which the Belfast punk scene was different from every other punk scene at the time. The Sex Pistols proclaimed there was "No Future" in England while the Ramones advocated "sniffin' glue" to deal with the monotony of American culture. The Stiff Little Fingers gave voice to the Belfast punks' desire to escape their parents' crushing sectarianism and work for a better, more peaceful world. It was a call for positivity and action over nihilism and passivity.

The B-side of the single featured the significantly lesser "78 RPM." Another Jake composition, he employed the title as a metaphor operating on multiple levels. In addition to a reference to older vinyl records being played at seventy-eight revolutions per minute, the chorus also called for revolutionary change. Each line dealt with a year of the Troubles, starting with 1969 and culminating in 1978, with an optimistic hope that the "new year" would bring an end to the fighting. The song also offered a biting response to the view being articulated by the British government at the time that the violence in Northern Ireland was at "acceptable levels." Finally, it rejected the view that punk had peaked in 1977 and run its course. With so much going on, the song sags under its muddled lyrical intentions. Musically, the song was a blatant rip-off of Rudi's hit "Big Time."[48] Filler at best, the band would wisely leave the song off of *Inflammable Material* a few months later.

Yet, major record labels continued to ignore the band, despite having two singles championed by radio DJ John Peel and aggressive promotion by their managers. After the calamitous brush with Island Records, other majors showed little interest in signing the Stiffs. Regardless, their popularity continued to grow, strengthened by a UK tour opening for the Tom Robinson Band. At one of these shows, Rough Trade's Geoff Travis offered to release a full-length album by the band. At the end of the tour, the band decided to take him up on the offer. The deal was sealed by a handshake, with an agreement that all profits would be split 50/50 after the label recouped its recording costs. This represented an incredibly generous offer, unheard of within the realm of major record labels. But it came with a risk: theirs would be Rough Trade's first full-length LP release.

For the first two weeks of November 1978, Rough Trade booked time at the Spaceward Studios in Cambridge, England. To keep costs down, they decided to forego a professional producer. Instead, in keeping with the label's DIY ethos, production was handled by Travis (whose studio experience had been limited to helping re-mix the "Alternative Ulster" single) and musician Mayo Thompson of Red Crayola/Red Krayola. Mike Kemp, owner of Spaceward Studios, and Gary Lucas both engineered the recordings.

Spaceward had just opened and only charged £200/day. The studio was a small, converted cellar on Clarendon Street, connected to another small, converted cellar on Victoria Street, which served as the control room. As Ali recalled, "It was damp, dark and cramped."[49] With little recording experience between them, Travis and Thompson wisely decided to capture the band's live sound and energy by having them set up in their on-stage formation and run through the original songs of their live set. As Jake recalls, "It really was just a case of setting up much like we did on stage and playing the songs through. I think the fact that Geoff and Mayo also had no real idea what they were doing helped ensure that the record came out sounding as rough and raw as it did."[50] The album took less than two weeks to record and mix. Both producers recall the band being very disciplined and focused, with no drinking and few distractions. As Mayo noted, "I recall how ready they were. They knew their material sideways."[51]

There are two points worth mentioning for listeners familiar with modern recording technology. First, they did not utilize a click track to ensure the band maintained a constant rhythm. Therefore, several songs on the album speed up as Brian's drumming propels the band forward with increasing energy. Second, there were no guitar tuners to keep the band in what is known as "concert pitch." Since the early twentieth century, the standard has been A440, meaning the note A above middle C is tuned to a frequency of 440 Hz. For the recording session, the band just tuned their guitars and bass to each other. As Henry recalls, "We just tuned to whoever's guitar sounded in tune. It was just a case of, 'Are you in tune? Right? We'll tune to that.'"[52] This made it nearly impossible to add guitar overdubs later (allegedly there are only two overdubs on the whole album). It also meant virtually every song on the album is technically "out of tune" (so if you are playing along, you'll be forgiven for thinking you are out of tune yourself).

While the recording process generally went smoothly, the band was already aware that major changes were afoot. Pressured by his fiancée to settle down and start a career, Brian had earlier informed the others of his intention to leave the band. The news did not come as a complete surprise. Knowing he was considering leaving, the band had been trying to convince Brian to stay for months. Throughout the fall tour with the Tom Robinson Band, his bandmates and those on the TRB crew all sought to talk Brian into staying in the band. As Jake recalls, "We spent a lot of time trying to talk him out of it . . . but he'd made his mind up and fair enough, you've got to respect his decision."[53] In addition to the pressure from his fiancée, Brian didn't enjoy touring and felt certain the band had run its course.[54] He agreed to stay long enough to record the album but insisted on being paid as a session drummer instead of taking a royalty cut because he didn't think the album would do well.

He would quickly be proven wrong. The album cost £2,000 to record. By the end of 1979, it had grossed over £250,000.[55] Under the original terms of the agreements with Rough Trade, splitting the profits 50/50, and the band's management, where profit was divided six ways, Brian would have made over £20,000 from *Inflammable Material* in its first year.

4
The Songs of *Inflammable Material* in the Context of the Troubles

"Suspect Device"

Inflammable Material starts with a re-recording of the band's first single, whose opening lyric provides the album's title. The Stiffs' decision to re-record "Suspect Device" proved to be a wise one as the original sounds slightly sluggish in comparison. Clocking in eight seconds shorter at two minutes thirty-six seconds, the album version also sounds fuller and exudes an air of greater urgency than the single version. And while the vocals might be slightly more intelligible on the original, Jake replaces the "make sure we get sod all" from the single with a more biting "fuck all" that hits harder—but also guarantees this version would not enjoy any radio airplay. With better production, a more spirited performance, and an angrier vocal delivery, the album version is superior to the still-impressive single.

"State of Emergency"

A few weeks before the fateful meeting with Gordon and Colin, in which Gordon presented him with the complete lyrics to "Suspect Device," Jake had been inspired by The Clash's first album to write about his own experiences in Belfast. As he recalled, "up to that point, I'd been singing other people's songs about bowling down Californian highways when I'd never been further west than Galway in my life. To suddenly hear guys singing about growing up in working-class West London showed me that you can write songs about that."[1] Though lyrically inspired by The Clash, musically the song reflected Jake's love of pub rock. The opening riffs of "State of Emergency" wouldn't have been out of place on an Eddie and The Hot Rods album. Regardless, "State of Emergency" stands as the first original Stiff Little Fingers' song.

Citizens of Northern Ireland had been effectively living in a state of emergency since the creation of the country. Upon the partition of the island, the government of Northern Ireland passed the 1922 Special Powers Act, empowering them to "take all such steps and issue all such orders as may be necessary for preserving the peace and maintaining order." This emergency legislation, renewed repeatedly until made permanent in 1933, enabled the government to impose any policy it deemed necessary, including indefinite internment. It was used almost exclusively against the minority nationalist population. In August 1971, in response to the growing civil rights movement and under the aegis of the Special Powers Act, the governments of Northern Ireland and the UK collectively directed the British Army to launch "Operation Demetrius," a two-day operation that saw troops carrying out waves of violent raids resulting in the arrest of 342 people. All were from Catholic nationalist backgrounds. Authorities did not detain a single person from a loyalist background. The operation resulted in a massive spike in violence, with over 7,000 people made homeless as houses were burned to the ground. Across Belfast, security forces established roadblocks to protect neighborhoods, while paramilitary violence from both sides greatly increased. In Belfast, the first battalion of a British parachute regiment killed eleven unarmed civilians in what became known as the Ballymurphy Massacre. A few months later, the same battalion opened fire on unarmed marchers in Derry, shooting twenty-six, in an incident known as Bloody Sunday. The following year, the British government imposed Direct Rule, dissolving the Parliament of Northern Ireland and ruling directly from London. They replaced the Special Powers Act with the Northern Ireland (Emergency Provisions) Act, maintaining the permanent state of emergency across the country.

By the time Jake sat down to write "State of Emergency," the situation had ossified into a new status quo. As Fionna McCann observed, "Over time, the abnormality of all this morphed into normalcy, even when it was contested (discursively or violently), and state propaganda ensured that the blame for all of these restrictions was firmly laid at the door of republican and loyalist paramilitaries, while the British state was presented as a benevolent peace-broker."[2] Yet, this song represents an interesting act of discursive contestation, in large part because it speaks directly to the listener, putting the onus of change on them. In the first verse, Jake challenges the listener: "You look for solutions but hate has made you blind / You keep looking 'round you for something that's in your mind / And you've spent the last ten years of your life in this emergency." In this telling, the problem isn't so much the repressive powers-that-be, but the average citizen's hatred. Rather than critiquing the authorities, Jake makes the listener culpable. But in the second verse, he offers solidarity within his call for action: "So please, just don't sit there / Let's try to break out from all the hatred, suspicion and doubt / Try to change your life that is no life at all." Failure to do so, Jake warns, will result in the listener being perpetually stuck "in this emergency."

Beyond the vague reference to "the last ten years," the song could easily be a general critique of "hatred" accompanied by a call for engagement and self-improvement. Listeners from outside Northern Ireland would be forgiven for not recognizing this as one of the handful of Belfast-informed songs on the album. But for those in Northern Ireland, this song was one of a few in circulation challenging the status quo, even if framed in terms of individual responsibility rather than offering a structural critique.

"Here We Are Nowhere"

By far the shortest song on the album, coming in under a minute, "Here We Are Nowhere" represents Henry's first contribution to the band. Lyrically, it is a classic bored-with-nothing-to-do punk song in the same vein as The Clash's

"London's Burning" or the first verse of "Alternative Ulster." Many observers—including Jake in several interviews—have suggested the title was a nod to Neil Young's 1969 song and album "Everybody Knows This Is Nowhere." But Henry denies this, claiming the title was just a phrase stuck in his head when he sat down to compose the song. As for the length, Henry observes: "I wrote a song and made sure it had three verses, three choruses, a bridge, and a guitar solo. So, I thought, 'Well, that's a song.' And then, it turned out to be 57 seconds long!"[3] Jake's snarly vocal delivery adds a welcome dose of menace to a teen-angst song of bored frustration.

"Wasted Life"

Civil unrest in Northern Ireland markedly increased in 1968 as the authorities responded to the civil rights movement with violent repression. Some of the worst rioting occurred in August 1969 around the annual Apprentice Boys march in Derry. After three days of rioting, commonly referred to as the "Battle of the Bogside," the British government agreed to deploy troops across Northern Ireland as part of "Operation Banner" (an operation that would last until July 2007). By the time the band began performing as Stiff Little Fingers, there were roughly 21,000 British soldiers in Northern Ireland. Officially, they were there to support the Royal Ulster Constabulary (RUC) and engage in counter-insurgency actions against the various paramilitaries. Yet, there is substantial evidence of collaboration with some loyalist groups. At that time, the security forces were facing an estimated 1,500 members of the nationalist Irish Republican Army (IRA), roughly 30,000 members of the unionist Ulster Defense Association (UDA), and another 1,500 members of the Ulster Volunteer Forces (UVF).[4]

"Wasted Life" opens with an A chord ringing out. As the note fades, Jake snarls, "I could be a soldier / Go out there and fight to save this land." The rest of the band joins in to thrash out a G chord before dropping out. Jake continues, "Be a people's soldier / Paramilitary gun in hand." And with those two opening lines, the gauntlet is thrown. The band isn't taking sides in the conflict. It is indicting all participants: the British army and paramilitary forces of both unionist and loyalist stripes. As the song propels forward, Jake leans into his anger, refusing to be a soldier, refusing to take orders. And in case his intentions aren't clear, he closes the verse with: "Stuff their fucking armies / Killing isn't my idea of fun."

Originally released as the B-side of "Suspect Device," "Wasted Life" is one of the most scathing songs on *Inflammable Material*. In the second verse, Jake mockingly sings of "heroes" who "live and die for their important cause," whether that cause is a "united nation or an independent state." In the third verse, he equates these fighters to Nazis, calling them "blind fascists." If Jake seemed reluctant to cast stones in "State of Emergency," he has no such reservations in "Wasted Life."

In one fell swoop, the band positioned themselves in opposition not just to the British army, but also against the various paramilitary forces. Within the context of the heightened violence and partisanship at the time, this entailed a powerful and potentially dangerous provocation.

Even the band's detractors conceded the point. As frequent critic Stuart Bailie observed, "They did have the balls, coming from the kind of place where you could be executed for saying something that certain gormless idiots didn't like or didn't approve of, to say those things. So in that sense ['Wasted Life'] was quite bold."[5] In 1976, a civilian was being killed almost every thirty hours. The threat of retaliation was real, and the Stiffs would have numerous gigs threatened with violence from various paramilitaries.

Jake credits Gordon for the inspiration and motivation to write the song. After Gordon handed him the lyrics to "Suspect Device," Jake went home to write the accompanying music but continued by writing the words and music to "Wasted Life" the same night. Jake quipped, "the song took as long to write as it takes to play it."[6] As he recalled, "Reading the 'Suspect Device' lyric had such a profound effect on me . . . From my point of view it almost gave me the 'permission' if you like, to release all the pent up aggravation I had lived through. Suddenly things I'd forgotten, like watching the local 'boys' at the start of the whole thing parading around with broom handles came back to the surface. The roadblocks, the riots, the constant hassle, in fact; the sheer paranoia of everyday life and how you almost felt suffocated by it, all this and more came tumbling out in 'Wasted Life.'"[7] While his personal experiences and frustrations fueled the lyrics, Jake explained in a March 1980 interview that the music was inspired by The Who's "Baba O'Reilly."[8]

While the song's verses are propelled by Jake's visceral anger, it's the chorus that hits hardest, reflecting on the huge societal cost of the Troubles. Speaking of the perpetrators of violence, Jake blames them for stealing his life away. When the Troubles began, the band members were all between the ages of ten and twelve. They came of age within that context, and two had been forced to flee their childhood homes to escape the violence. As Jake notes, "My life and the lives of everybody else of my generation and subsequent generations had been completely defined by what had been going on around us. We hadn't actually had our teenage years at all. We hadn't had any sort of growing-up experience—we'd either had to grow up very, very quickly or we hadn't been allowed to grow up at all. We hadn't been allowed to be kids."[9] As such, the song spoke not just to the loss of lives, but the deep traumas affecting all citizens of Northern Ireland. More than a song lamenting the deaths incurred, it raged against the incalculable cost of living in the Troubles.

Though the band feared "Wasted Life" wouldn't have much of an audience outside of Northern Ireland, they were repeatedly rewarded with kids telling them what a positive impact the song had on them. For example, Ali recalls one incident when they "met a couple of kids after a show who'd said that because of the influence of the band and the lyrics, they had thought twice about getting involved in the local paramilitaries. All party politics aside, that could have been a couple of lives saved."[10] Jake has observed, "I know that probably out of all the songs I've written that one has probably had the most effect or the most influence of them all. Others have probably had better tunes or better guitar licks but that one was probably the most honest song that I've ever written."[11] The demo version that graced the B-side of "Suspect Device" was a spirited affair, completed in two takes with a guitar flub included. But the re-recorded version on the album is a heftier, more moving rendition, superior in every way.

"No More of That"

Henry's second contribution to *Inflammable Material* is his critique of life during the Troubles, in which he also features on lead vocals. "No More of That" is primarily a complaint about the disempowerment of the average citizen opposed to the conflict. The song opens with the observation that no one was ever asked if they wanted war, and for two minutes is propelled by the chorus of, "We want no more of that / You can't push us under the mat / Oh, we want no more of that."

While certainly not the strongest song on the album, it has been unduly dismissed by others. In one interview, Jake shrugged off "No More of That" as lacking "any great depth."[12] When the band first recorded the song in April 1978 for John Peel's influential radio show, Gordon undermined its chance of being broadcast when, in the letter he wrote to Peel accompanying the session recordings, he described it as "pretty much a throwaway number that we just had time for."[13] When asked about those responses, Henry self-deprecatingly observed, "You're probably asking the wrong person, because one thing I've always done if I write a song, after five minutes, I don't like it. So, for anybody to say it was a throwaway song, fair enough. It doesn't bother me. But nobody comes up and talks to me about *Inflammable Material* and says, 'I like every song apart from No More of That.'"[14] Though it spoke directly to the Troubles, the lyrics are vague enough that the song has had a life beyond Belfast, even becoming an anti-misogyny anthem for a women's rights organization in the UK.

"Barbed Wire Love"

Reacting to their growing media reputation as the Voice of the Troubles, the band chose to write a ridiculously silly song that took the piss out of the conflict and mocked their own seriousness. The result was a ballad of sorts, complete with a doo-wop breakdown, about two star-crossed lovers finding each other across the barricades.

Gordon has claimed to be the primary motivator behind the song, wanting to lighten the tone of the band with an ironic love ballad. Gordon and Jake often wrote separately, providing each other with almost completed lyrics, but the two composed "Barbed Wire Love" together in Gordon's flat. They aimed to come up with as many outrageous puns related to the Troubles as they could. Jake recalls,

> When we wrote "Barbed Wire Love" we were in the middle of writing the first batch of songs . . . We knew that a lot of people were going to level a lot of these criticisms against us saying, "You've no sense of humour, you're always writing about the Troubles." So we gathered together as many clichés as we could find or reference points to our own songs at that point and put them all in to one song and basically took the piss out of ourselves.[15]

One of the more outrageous puns was the line "you set my ArmaLite," a reference to the ArmaLite assault rifle popular among paramilitary forces. But for listeners outside Northern Ireland, the line has occasionally been mistaken as a drug reference. As Henry observed, "We got people who would say, 'Is it about drugs? You set my arm alight?' People don't know what an ArmaLite is, which is fair enough—why should you?"[16] Despite being weighed down by terrible puns, the song manages to work, largely due to its catchy chorus and the surprising revelation of the band's sense of humor.

"White Noise"

Arguably the most ill-conceived song on the album is "White Noise," meant to be an ironic anti-racist missive. The lyrics, written mostly by Ogilvie (again, an English journalist), consist entirely of racist tropes common in right-wing rhetoric. The first verse is a collection of anti-Black slurs and the second of anti-Asian ones. The chorus alternates between attacking "black wogs" and "brown wogs," proclaiming "your face don't fit . . . you ain't no Brit!" These lyrics reproduced familiar racist hatred, made more visceral by Jake's angry snarling delivery. The supposed ironic twist comes in the third verse when Jake switches to attacking "green wogs" and enumerating various anti-Irish tropes. Jake explained, "Being Irish ourselves, that was supposed to highlight the irony within the song."[17] Yet such anti-Irish rhetoric was common among unionists who identified as "British" rather than "Irish." If listeners missed Jake's proclamation, "We ain't no Brits" in the final chorus, they could be forgiven for thinking the band was indulging in racist bile.

The song was originally intended for inclusion on a Northern Ireland Rock Against Racism LP that never materialized.[18] Activists founded Rock Against Racism (RAR) in 1976, partly in response to Eric Clapton's racist comments about immigrants at a Birmingham concert that August. It also represented a reaction to the rise of right-wing groups like the National Front (NF) in the UK and the growth of right-wing related street violence across the UK. RAR collaborated with the Anti-Nazi League, a coalition founded in August 1977 after anti-fascist forces forcibly stopped a National Front march in Lewisham. In addition to offering the song for the unrealized compilation, the Stiffs played at several Rock Against Racism shows.

Assuming their anti-racist beliefs were beyond reproach, the band has repeatedly expressed shock and surprise that some listeners missed the ironic intention of the song. Ali recalls: "A lot of people did take it the wrong way, even to the extent that we were getting write ups in fascist magazines."[19] During performances of the song, some audience members would throw Nazi salutes in front of the band.[20] At one show at The Harp, a group of NF supporters started doing the Nazi salute inches from Jake's face before punching him in the jaw.[21] The band would run into the same problem of misinterpreted intentions with "Fly the Flag" off their second LP, *Nobody's Heroes*. What was intended to be an ironic mocking of nationalism, complete with a musical reference to "Rule Britannia," ended up being embraced and championed by various National Front magazines.

In Newcastle upon Tyne, a local councilor of Pakistani origin heard "White Noise," reputedly from his daughter, and took it at face value. Raising the issue in the council chamber, the councilor managed to get the band banned from playing in the city for two years. The local press covered the story with the headline "PUNK ALBUM COULD START NORTH EAST RACE RIOT."[22] Jake notes that, "Nobody came to us and asked us for a comment on this so we were hung, drawn and quartered without being given the chance to defend ourselves."[23] Ironically, the photograph the local paper used to accompany their article captured the band performing in front of a huge banner reading "Rock Against Racism."

"Breakout"

Often assumed to be a lament about being stuck in Belfast, "Breakout" was the second song Jake wrote when he was working as an accounts clerk with Mackie Engineering, one of the largest employers in Belfast. As he recalls, "I was stuck in what I saw as a dead-end job and didn't want to be there." Referencing The Clash, he notes, "It was the standard 'career opportunities' type song: 'I'm stuck in a dead-end job, I'm bored, I'm fed up and I don't want to be fucking doing it anymore' . . . It wasn't at all politically inspired or about anything that people might want to read into it, saying I was trying to get away from Belfast—I was trying to get away from an accounts office."[24]

By Jake's own admission, the song is hugely inspired by Eddie and The Hot Rods' "Do Anything You Wanna Do," both musically and lyrically. That song opens with the verse: "Gonna break out of the city / Leave the people here behind / Searching for adventure / It's the type of life to find." These lines are slightly reworked by Jake for the chorus of "Breakout," as he sings: "Break out and leave this life behind / Break out and see what I can find." Featuring some nice bass work by Ali, it is neither the strongest nor weakest song on the album, but an admirable closer for the first side.

"Law and Order"

In the late 1970s, punks faced regular harassment just for being punks. From London to New York City, it was not unusual for punks to be targeted by police for the way they looked. Tales of police harassment were rife in Belfast, a city with a significant police and army presence. In a March 1978 interview with *NME*, Jake quipped, "Punks in England complain about hassles in the street . . . but they've never seen hooded men at a barricade. Their cops don't carry submachine guns."[25] "Law and Order" is based on a particular experience of one of Jake's friends, but just about everyone in the Belfast punk scene would have had similar stories of harassment and abuse at the hands of the authorities.

The song opens with Jake observing that "everybody" is in the center of town, "doing nothing wrong" and "only hangin' around." In the context of 1978 Belfast, the "everybody" clearly referred to punks, who would often be the only ones found in the no-man's land of the barricade-encircled city center after dark. In Jake's telling, the police arrive to "put you up against the wall" and "laugh at your appearance and the clothes you wear." But the tone in the second verse turns darker and more violent, as Jake enumerates the violence enacted upon his friend, from pulled hair to being kicked in the head.

During the Troubles, the RUC was one of the world's most dangerous police forces to serve in, with 319 officers killed and over 9,000 injured, mostly by IRA paramilitary forces.[26] It was also an institution of considerable corruption and brutality. In "Law and Order," what begins as a typical punk complaint against police harassment transforms into something more menacing given the Belfast context. As Jake noted later, "Of course, it was magnified a hundred times by being in Belfast because they had the right to stop and search you for no reason just because they didn't like the look of you, so we were regularly getting stopped and 'Give us your name and address' and all that. ["Law and Order"] was just a reaction to that and also to the horror stories you'd hear about friends who had been arrested and had been given a good kicking for no damn reason."[27]

"Law and Order" was surely inspired by Rudi's "Cops," a popular Belfast punk anthem written about the "Battle of Bedford Street," when cops and punks scuffled after the cancelled Clash gig. Rudi's song is anchored by the chorus "We hate cops" and opens and closes with a chant of "SS RUC." It is hard to imagine Gordon and Jake did not intend to write a similar song to compete with their Belfast rivals. And while "Law and Order" is far inferior to Rudi's "Cops," it did benefit from being professionally recorded in a studio while the latter never was.

"Rough Trade"

In the grand tradition of punk bands slagging off their record labels—see The Clash's "Complete Control" and the Sex Pistols' "EMI"—the Stiffs offered their own blistering missive with "Rough Trade." Given the title, listeners could be forgiven for assuming the band was singing about their own label. But the target of their wrath was Island Records, with the title drawing from the euphemism for male prostitution to characterize the larger music industry.

The band was initially devastated after Island CEO Chris Blackwell rescinded their contract offer at the eleventh hour. Jake and Brian had both quit their day jobs, and the debacle was likely the final straw for Brian. But after the initial setback, Jake poured his anger into writing "Rough Trade." Jake recalls, "We'd been had over by Island Records and being the petulant young man I was, I went away and wrote a song about it. Not really important in the great scheme of things, but very important to us at the time."[28] Despite the vitriol evident in the lyrics (the chorus is "We were betrayed by lies!") the song is neither the angriest nor most spirited on the album, but definitely a better-than-average contribution.

It isn't entirely true that "Rough Trade" has nothing to do with their label of the same name. Towards the end of the song, Jake promises revenge against the music industry hacks in their "London office, smug and warm." Referring to the good folks at Rough Trade, who had agreed to put out the "Alternative Ulster" single and the *Inflammable Material* album, Jake sings: "We're gonna do it our way / We're gonna make it on our own / 'Cause we've found people to trust /

People who put music first." Later, Jake and others in the band would maintain that Island Records did them a favor. First, it taught them valuable lessons about the music business and the need to persevere. Second, they ended up with a far more lucrative deal with Rough Trade thanks to the 50/50 profit-sharing deal. Finally, they all agree the original Island demos sounded restrained, suggesting any album on that label would likely also be watered down. As Jake observed, "I don't think we'd have been allowed to make such a ferociously angry record anywhere else."[29] Jake's praise of the Rough Trade label is slightly ironic given what will transpire in a few short months.

"Johnny Was"

Henry claims to have brought reggae music into the band's consciousness after he bought Bob Marley's *Exodus*. The band became intent on covering a reggae song after hearing The Clash's cover of Junior Murvin's "Police and Thieves." Gordon suggested Bob Marley's "Johnny Was" from *Rastaman Vibration*.

Credited to Marley's wife Rita, the original song is a slow, loping lament narrated by the grieving mother of a son killed by a stray bullet during the unrest gripping Kingston, Jamaica. Concerned that her son might not get to heaven, the distraught mother repeatedly proclaims, "he was a good man." Marley released the song in early 1976 as social unrest swept the Caribbean island. By year's end, more than a hundred civilians had been killed across Jamaica and the major political parties were forming paramilitary forces. Parallels with Northern Ireland were striking.

1976 turned out to be the second deadliest year of the Troubles, with 297 deaths reported. Three years later, when *Inflammable Material* was released, the death rate had decreased to only one death every three days.[30] Almost every year, attacks and killings spiked during the summer's so-called "marching season." In Northern Ireland, during the months from April to August, Protestant groups, such as the Apprentice Boys of Derry and the Orange Order, celebrate Prince William of Orange's victory over King James at the Battle of the Boyne in 1690 with public parades. Often provocatively marching through Catholic neighborhoods, these parades typically feature fife and drum marching bands.

As the Stiffs were working up their cover of "Johnny Was," Brian started playing the military drumbeat familiar across Northern Ireland from Protestant parades. It may have been Brian's most important contribution to the band. After that inspired innovation, everything fell into place. The band relocated the scene of Johnny's death to Northern Ireland— "a single shot rings out in a Belfast night"—with Brian's opening snare beats evoking the marching season. Listening to The Clash's version of "Police and Thieves," Jake noticed they had taken the top guitar line and made it the bassline. He decided to flip the approach and convert the bass line of Marley's original into the guitar line, emphasizing the discord to emulate automatic fire.[31] Once included in their live performances, the cover quickly became the heart of the set, with the band often stretching it out for maximum impact.

In the studio, Jake insists, "That was the one track on the record we were determined to get right, probably because it was somebody else's song but also because we knew by that stage it had already become a centre piece of the set and it was also going to be centre piece of the album." After cutting his vocal take, Jake wanted to know if anybody in the control room had cried. When they responded in the negative, Jake replied, "Well, keep me singing until somebody cries," noting that, "We were that desperate to try and convey the emotion that we felt was in the song."[32] Clocking in at over eight minutes, it is by far the LP's longest song, and true to the band's intent, provides the album's heart.

"Alternative Ulster"

The band wisely chose to use the remixed version of "Alternative Ulster" they had already released as a single. Why screw with perfection? And it is worth recalling that the recording was originally intended to just be a demo for Island Records.

Coming on the heels of "Johnny Was," it should have closed the album to maximum effect. Unfortunately, the band was talked into including one more song.

"Closed Groove"

Never has anyone claimed "Closed Groove" as their favorite Stiff Little Fingers' song.

It is not controversial to state that *Inflammable Material* would be a superior album without "Closed Groove." Yet, Gordon Ogilvie believed the album was not long enough and insisted the band include his recently penned "Closed Groove." The song is not only unnecessary but is stylistically different—jarringly so—from everything that comes before. Supposedly intended to sound like an XTC song, Jake further muddied the waters by singing in a fake Cockney accent: "I couldn't get Ian Dury's voice out of my head, which is why I pronounce the 'what' as 'wot' all the way through it."[33]

Employing an answering machine as a metaphor and gimmick, the song's title references the closed-mindedness of the narrator but also the run-out groove of a vinyl record. When *Inflammable Material* was pressed, the run-out groove was designed to make the needle perpetually skip backwards (hence, a closed groove), so that it would end with the infinite repeating of a ringing telephone (it didn't always work). A weak offering by everyone's estimation, Henry considers the song "bloody awful. Probably the biggest waste of space we ever recorded."[34]

5
After Lighting the Match
SLF's Troubled Relationship with Belfast Punk

Rough Trade released *Inflammable Material* on February 2, 1979, the day the band began a package tour with label mates Essential Logic and Robert Rental & The Normal. Reviews of the album were immediately positive. Garry Bushell at *Sounds* gave the LP five stars, calling it: "A magnificent slice of vintage punk played fast and frantic, and loaded with powerful lyrics and forceful hooks barked out with anger and conviction."[1] Over at the *New Musical Express*, Paul Morley wrote, "*Inflammable Material* is the classic punk rock record . . . There are parts . . . that are not just exciting or stimulating but quite humbling. It is a remarkable document."[2] While Chris Westwood of the *Record Mirror* criticized the lyrics for being "reactionary, hypertensive mock-shock socialism," he concluded the album "outguns the first Pistols' album, the first Ramones' album, both Clash albums. Ferocious, blinding, madcap, overdrive . . . The sound is vibrant, coarse, all encompassing, unrestricted."[3]

On 21 February, which happened to be Jake's twenty-first birthday, the album entered the UK's national chart at #14. The album sold over 20,000 copies in a few short weeks. In addition to being commercially successful, *Inflammable Material* achieved an important historic milestone—it became the first totally independent release to ever enter the UK's Top 20 album chart. Remarkably, up to that point, Rough Trade had not spent a single penny on advertising the album.[4] The band and label were both completely caught off guard by the album's success. Driven by the band's growing popularity, audiences for the Rough Trade package tour outpaced the size of the venues booked. The tour was intended to feature a rotating line-up, but it quickly became apparent audiences expected the Stiffs to headline.

But the Stiffs had literally become a different band. True to his word, Brian quit soon after the recording sessions ended. In December 1978, months before *Inflammable Material* was released, the Stiffs posted ads in various music magazines looking for a new drummer. One day they received a call at the Rough Trade office from a young man who introduced himself with, "Hi, I'm your new drummer." Originally from Belfast, Jim Reilly was living in Sheffield at the time. At the audition, he impressed the band with his drumming skills and knowledge of many of their songs. Plus, he seemed to get along well with the more taciturn Henry, which sealed the deal. Only afterward did they realize Reilly had sold his drum kit to pay for his train ticket from Sheffield to London for the audition.[5]

Reilly hailed from a Catholic background, which finally gave truth to Gordon's continuing claim that the band consisted of a mix of Catholics and Protestants. As Siobhan Fahey, founder of Bananarama and Jim's then-girlfriend, observed, "It was great politically for Stiff Little Fingers when Jim joined the group because he was the real deal. He added credibility to the early image the Stiffs had promoted, wherein they'd claimed to have been a band from both sides of the divide. Whereas the others were a little bit middle class Jim really had grown up in a Catholic ghetto in Turf Lodge, West Belfast."[6] Despite Gordon's regular promotion of the band as mixed, the band often resisted commenting on the members' political or religious backgrounds. In a 1978 interview, Jake claimed: "When 'Suspect Device' came out we had a full-page spread in the Irish edition of the *Daily Mirror* where they just about said we were Republicans. Then the *NME* described us as Loyalists. No one knew where the hell we were coming from which is great."[7]

Media attention on the band greatly increased with the release of their album. As Roland Link observed in his biography of the band, "By the end of February . . . Stiff Little Fingers were the new, undisputed darlings of the British music press."[8] Ali would later observe in an October 1982 interview, "Looking back I think the reviews were too good. We were lucky in that we came along at the right time. I mean, everybody saw this album and said, 'Here it is, a real punk album,' because everybody was starting to get a little bit skeptical, a little bit cynical after the first excesses of punk from the Sex Pistols and the Damned and so on. People had thought how far can they take this? This is not what it was supposed to be about originally, and then we came along and they said, 'Ah, a punk band with a proper cause,' because we were from Belfast and we wrote songs about Belfast, nobody else had written songs that you could get so angry about."[9]

The Belfast connection became central to the marketing of the band. Gordon had always maintained the Stiffs needed an angle to set them apart from all the other bands flooding the market and continued to employ sensationalist rhetoric and shock value tactics to achieve this. Such moves increased the view back home that they exploited the Troubles for their own advancement. They were also the first band from the Belfast punk scene to release a full-length album. Rudi's debut single "Big Time" hit the shelves in April 1978 while the Undertones from Derry released "Teenage Kicks" on 21 October (days after the release of "Alternative Ulster"), both on the fledgling Good Vibrations record label of Terri Hooley. With the release of *Inflammable Material*, Stuart Bailie recalls, "All of a sudden there was this howl of derision from the first real punks in Northern Ireland that Stiff Little Fingers had somehow gatecrashed the party and jumped ahead of everybody else. Of course, Northern Ireland was also the most argumentative place in the world at the time. It didn't take long for their hometown fans to turn against them."[10]

While Stiff Little Fingers were being sold to the world on the back of their supposed war-torn street cred, their relationship with the Belfast scene became increasingly complicated and fraught. What's more, just as the band started its upward trajectory, the Belfast punk scene grew in strength and importance, becoming the most vital and politically significant scene in the world. But the band was largely absent from the developments taking place. Even before *Inflammable Material* was released, the band (except Henry) relocated to London and consciously decided to stop writing about Belfast.

The Importance of the Belfast Punk Scene

While London punks rebelled primarily against the stifling commercial culture of Britain in the late 1970s, the punks in Northern Ireland had to contend with the stifling culture of sectarianism that had ripped apart their society. For years, young people had been forced into opposing camps. Punk was a response to that violent divisiveness. John T. Davis captured the emerging Belfast scene in his 1979 documentary *Shellshock Rock*.[11] The film, filmed mostly in late summer/autumn 1978, offers an insightful snapshot of the ways in which the Belfast punks were driven by an anti-status quo philosophy, a rejection of conformity and their parents' culture. Having flown back from London to play a gig for the cameras, the Stiffs feature prominently in the documentary (even though they had effectively vacated the scene by that point). In one clip, the band explicitly states that the core principle of the Belfast punk scene is a rejection of sectarianism.

Punk in Northern Ireland actively challenged the religious, political, and social forces driving sectarianism. As media scholar Martin McLoone noted, in Northern Ireland, "Punk music and the punk scene in general is all about giving an identity to the young that would allow them to come together with a shared set of cultural beliefs and tastes that are beyond religious and political norms."[12] Young punks echo this sentiment over and over again in *Shellshock Rock*, driving home the point that the Belfast punk scene established safe, non-sectarian spaces for Northern Irish youths.

Interestingly, the physical spaces punks staked out were in the city center, which had become deserted at night by everyone except the security forces. As the Stiffs referenced in "Law and Order," the abandoned city center provided a meeting place where punks could come together outside the sectarian pressures of their home housing estates. One of the most important spaces proved to be an old pub called The Harp. Upstairs held a 300-person room with a dance floor described by Gavin Martin as "the size of two double-beds placed side by side."[13] Local punks started booking shows at The Harp in early 1978, and it soon became ground zero for the scene. Days after recording their Island Records demos, SLF returned to Belfast to play their debut gig at the Harp on May 27, 1978, with the Androids.

Another major meeting place for local punks became Terri Hooley's Good Vibrations record store on Great Victoria Street. Hooley had been a local fixture for years. He became a rabid punk convert after being dragged to The Pound for a gig on January 12, 1978, featuring Rudi and The Outcasts. Hooley was completely taken by Rudi, who were in discussions with the editors of *Alternative Ulster* to include a free Rudi flexidisc in an upcoming issue. The zine was published by Dave and Marily Hyndman in their Print Workshop located above Hooley's record store. The band and editors approached Hooley to help price the cost of pressing the flexi. When he discovered it would cost only slightly more to press a vinyl version of the single, Hooley suggested he release it himself, despite having no experience running a record label. In typical DIY punk fashion, Hooley established the Good Vibrations label and began releasing a torrent of punk singles from Northern Ireland, some highly influential (such as Rudi's "Big Time" and The Undertones' "Teenage Kicks") and others less so. Hooley is a larger-than-life character who has had an outsized impact on Northern Irish music and culture. Roland Link offers an apt description of Hooley: "Idealistic to the point of ruin, enthusiastic to the point of mania, he was (and still is), above all else a massive music fan."[14]

For a time, Hooley and friends organized a weekly "Punk Workshop" at The Harp. However, most bands booked their own gigs directly through Maureen, the bar manager or her assistant Tony. By summer 1978, the venue hosted regular punk shows on Friday and Saturday nights, with a "punk disco" on Thursdays. By then, the three original punk bands (Rudi, Outcasts, and SLF) had been joined by numerous other punk bands such as Roofwrecks (later Ruefrex), Victim, Pretty Boy Floyd and The Gems (the punk alter-ego/ reinvention of showband Candy), Protex Blue (eventually becoming just Protex), and the Androids. In short order, they would be joined by the Idiots, Stage B, Sub Standards, Batteries, Producers (who eventually became Ex-Producers), and Moondogs from Derry, to name but a few. As Brian Young of Rudi recalls, "Dozens of bands all emerged once the Harp provided a venue. We'd always lend any band who were playing with us our back line/PA. So, the competition was fierce, and it kept you on your toes."[15]

The punk scene in Belfast differed from other emerging scenes in important ways. Demographically, it was significantly younger, largely created by and for teenagers. There are numerous tales of punks in the London and New York scenes lying about their age and obscuring their previous history of playing in hippie or rock bands (The Clash being the most obvious but far from the only example). At the time, the Belfast scene was also largely devoid of hard drugs, given that the paramilitaries violently disavowed them. And while being a punk in 1970s London or New York City might earn you stares and possibly verbal abuse, the stakes were much higher in Belfast. As photographer Ricky Adam observed, "Being a punk, especially in a city like Belfast, was a political statement in itself."[16] This was largely because the social landscape was already highly politicized. As Stuart Bailie would later quip, "Even the decision to have fun during those wretched years was a political act."[17] Writing about the politics of popular music, political scientist John Street observed: "Whether pop is banal or brilliant, it is political because it affects or reflects the way people behave. It may make little difference to the way they vote, but votes make little difference to the way politicians behave. What it affects or reinforces are the politics of the everyday."[18]

One of the ways Belfast punks affected the "politics of the everyday" was by creating relatively safe, non-sectarian spaces at places such as The Harp and Pound. Along with Hooley's Good Vibrations record store, these spaces provided the material infrastructure around which the scene coalesced. In these spaces, connections were made and communities were built. Scenes can function as conduits for collective action.

There is, after all, strength in numbers. Scenes serve to strengthen, protect, and nurture their members. In doing so, they create an emotional community that can help promote political activity. In the context of highly polarized Belfast, such connections and personal networks significantly altered the social landscape of the city. The importance of this development cannot be stressed enough.

Initially, what made a place like The Harp so important was its location in the city center, neutral ground where punks from across the sectarian divide could meet and socialize—something not happening elsewhere. Brian Young of Rudi recalls, "The importance of The Harp can't be underestimated. It was the first night-time venue in the city center where punks from all over the place could meet safely . . . and where it was the music you liked that mattered, not where you were from or what religion you were."[19] Recalling their own experiences at The Harp, Sean O'Neil and Guy Trelford claimed, "Punk kids from both sides of the religious divide, working class, middle class, and even the rich kids from Malone Road, mixed freely in the Harp without fear or intimidation, and drank alongside hoods, dockers and strippers."[20]

Of course, one shouldn't overly romanticize the situation. There were still fisticuffs and aggressive behavior. Not everyone felt safe in that space. Maureen Lawrence recalls, "It was very much a boys' club to begin with."[21] Moreover, sectarianism didn't disappear. As Greg Cowan of The Outcasts points out, "You don't take a guy who's sixteen, seventeen, eighteen years of age, who's been brought up in a very bigoted community and think he's going to walk in and go, 'Let's hug a Catholic.'"[22] But even with the preexisting baggage, Cowan and others note that punks created their own community. As Brian Young notes, "[At The Harp] You were a punk rocker first and foremost and everything else was secondary . . . any actual fisticuffs were generally more to do with your allegiance to a particular band or crowd, rather than along more usual sectarian lines."[23]

Just as importantly, in a city steeped in conflict and divisions, many punks worked hard to preserve that camaraderie and harmony. When the English band The Damned played in Belfast, the drummer Rat Scabies casually asked the audience which football team they supported. In the Northern Ireland context, team allegiance served as an indicator of sectarian identity. In response, the whole room fell silent rather than answer the question.[24] One participant of the Belfast scene reflects, "Suddenly you got to pick a side, you got to say this is who I am and my allegiances lie with punk and with the punks, they are my community you know. It's hard to get that across like in terms of how monumental that was, 'cause just no-one done it before that I knew of."[25] In another infamous example, Henry McDonald, an Irish journalist, accompanied a dozen young punks walking down a Belfast street at night when they were stopped by the police. After taking their names and addresses, McDonald reported the police officer couldn't believe the kids were from all across the sectarian-divided city and let the kids go, shaking his head in disbelief.[26]

The importance of the Belfast punk scene wasn't just about bringing the youth together. It also altered the discursive terrain within Belfast and Northern Ireland in general.

Just as the physical geography of the city was fragmented and policed by the state and the paramilitaries, symbols and words were highly charged and violently policed. The Union Jack, for example, was a required accoutrement in loyalist neighborhoods, but heretical in nationalist ones. As Anna Burns writes in her highly acclaimed 2018 novel *Milkman*, set during the Troubles: "As regards this psycho-political atmosphere, with its rules of allegiance, of tribal identification, of what was allowed and not allowed, matters didn't stop at 'their names' and at 'our names,' at 'us' and 'them,' at 'our community' and 'their community,' at 'over the road,' 'over the water,' and 'over the border.' Other issues had similar directives attaching as well . . . There was food and drink. The right butter. The wrong butter. The tea of allegiance. The tea of betrayal. There were 'our shops' and 'their shops.' Place names. What school you went to. What prayers you said. What hymns you sang. How you pronounced your 'haitch' or 'aitch.'"[27] Virtually everything within discourse, including popular culture, ended up saturated by the sectarian partisanship characterizing the Troubles.

Punk directly challenged both the polarization of discourse along sectarian lines, as well as the attempt to freeze meaning within each "tribe," to use Anna Burns' language. Take the earlier example of the Union Jack. This is not an inconsequential example, given that defacing the Union Jack or the image of the Queen was a common practice for punks in the London scene. But doing so could literally get you killed in Northern Ireland. There, defacing these symbols was regarded as an act of allegiance to the republican cause prior to the emergence of punk. But punk created an alternative space where new meaning-making practices were enacted. Defacing the symbols of power was no longer seen exclusively as acts of sectarianism but as pledging allegiance to an explicitly non-sectarian punk community.

Punk's challenge to, and restructuring of, the discursive status quo was an important, perhaps even necessary, development in the process of building a foundation for peace. As social theorist Alberto Melucci has argued, the status quo must first be challenged at the cultural level before mass collective action can occur. One must "challenge and overturn the dominant codes upon which social relationships are founded. These symbolic challenges are a method of unmasking the dominant codes, a different way of perceiving and naming the world."[28] Take for example, when punks in the audience would join the band Rudi in chanting "SS RUC!" at the beginning of their popular song "Cops." Within the discourse of the nationalist community, the Royal Ulster Constabulary was the symbolic representation and physical manifestation of oppressive colonial occupation. Within the loyalist discourse, the RUC functioned both as a symbol of patriotic allegiance and as a source of protection. But punks forced open a new, alternative discursive space. Everyone knew Rudi, a band from the Protestant side of town, was not pledging fealty to the IRA, but decrying the fascistic brutality of the RUC experienced by punks.[29]

Belfast punks' challenge to the discursive status quo was regarded as a serious threat by all sides of the conflict. These punks were frequently targeted by sectarian violence, which further intensified the sense of community. The Harp Bar's "Punk Workshop" committee arranged for groups of punks, destined for the same areas, to leave the club together, as traversing the city streets could be a highly hazardous experience.[30] There are numerous examples of gigs by the Stiffs, Rudi, Outcasts, and other punk bands being regularly threatened by the IRA, UDA, and other armed groups.[31] For his part, Terri Hooley was regularly threatened and occasionally assaulted by various paramilitaries "simply for bringing the kids together." As he muses, "What we were doing was a threat to their agendas and their twisted world views."[32] In Melucci's language, punk provided "symbolic challenges" to the "dominant codes" and, in so doing, created the language and symbols to imagine alternative ways of being within Belfast and Northern Ireland.

Punk provided Northern Irish youths with options and alternatives beyond the dominant binary of sectarianism. As Hooley observes, "Kids had a choice: join the paramilitaries or become punks. Punk saved a lot of lives."[33] But more than that, punk in Belfast explicitly promoted political and cultural empowerment for a marginalized and terrorized population. Belfast punks were not passive consumers, dreaming of a better life in the safety of their bedrooms. They were actively producing cultural forms that helped alter their surroundings and everyday lives. As punks redeployed symbols, language, and meanings in the discursive terrain of conflict-torn Belfast, they were creating alternative practices of meaning-making that challenged sectarianism.[34] They were constructing the means to imagine and realize alternative ways of being. Punks in Belfast were, in word and deed, working to create an "Alternative Ulster." Ironically, the band that had penned the anthem for this vision had relocated to London.

SLF's Difficult Relationship with Belfast Scene

As noted earlier, by the end of 1978, the Stiff Little Fingers crew, with the notable exception of Henry, had all moved away from Belfast. Though Henry frequently visited The Harp and witnessed the evolution of the Belfast punk scene discussed above, the other band members (Jake, Ali, and newcomer Jim) were living in London, as was Gordon, who had been transferred to the London office of the *Daily Express*. Colin and his family had moved to Dublin to take a job at the *Sunday World* newspaper. The band's exit from Belfast underscored the complicated relationship the band had with its hometown and the punk scene there. Earlier sites of contention, discussed briefly in chapter two, became more pronounced after the release of *Inflammable Material*.

Many local punks had long been suspicious of the band's *bona fides*, believing they were merely rock opportunists jumping on the punk bandwagon. For example, Tony McGartland of Omagh band Straightjackets dismissed them as a "heavy metal band dressed as punks."[35] Roy Wallace of Toxic Waste charged "[SLF] were wrapped up in all the music industry shit that swallowed up the whole punk philosophy and made it into a business with so many units to shift in the record shops each week."[36] It didn't help that the band made no bones about wanting to land a record deal and become famous. Speaking to Paul Morley in the *NME*, Jake was blunt about wanting to get out of Belfast: "I can't deny it. I mean there've always been three ways out, join the army, be a professional footballer, or be a rock'n'roll singer. In Belfast you just don't join the army, so you've only got two choices left; and we haven't got many great footballers . . . so it's down to becoming a rock'n'roll singer."[37] Later, Jake would observe, "Although we'd started out playing just for fun, we very quickly adopted a much more professional attitude to the whole thing. We had raw, naked ambition. We were very determined to do the thing properly and to succeed, which did garner us a certain amount of animosity."[38]

A fair amount of suspicion existed regarding the band's relationship with the two journalists who became their managers and, in Gordon's case, the co-writer of most of their lyrics. When he heard about the band's newly acquired management team, Dave McCullough (writing as "D. Angry") mused in *Alternative Ulster*, "we feel . . . that the shadowy business berks that bedevil the SLF backroom will inevitably hinder, cramp, and shorten the career of this excellent band. Such contingencies would be, to say the least, sad."[39] Writing in *Sounds*, Peter Silverton worried: "cynical Grub Street hacks [could be] manipulating a band into success, while simultaneously expressing some of the ideas that the dictates of their journalistic briefs make impossible to so much as mention in the papers that pay their salaries . . . And then when you see that Ogilvie gets a co-credit on the band's first single . . . you can't help but be very suspicious about exactly whose band Stiff Little Fingers is."[40] This criticism differed greatly from how the band regarded themselves. Jake, when discussing why the band chose not to keep things local and work with Terry Hooley's Good Vibration record label, explained, "From the very beginning the band made a conscious decision to be in charge of their destiny . . . We decided very much from the start that we were going to be our own bosses, going to be our own people."[41] Whenever asked about the influence of Gordon and Colin on the band, Henry has long maintained, "we were never anyone's puppets."[42]

Perhaps the primary criticism of the band was that it exploited the Troubles for their own benefit. This view had been articulated in the *Shellshock Rock* documentary when Aidan Murtagh, guitarist/singer of Protex, criticized the "political sloganeering" of Stiff Little Fingers: "We can't sing about Ulster. I'm fed up. We all live in it."[43] Years later, he would go on to say: "We did not want to write about the Troubles. I had people who've had experience of the Troubles. My family has. My family business has. And I really didn't want to be writing about it."[44]

Speaking directly about the Troubles opened Stiff Little Fingers up to numerous criticisms. Writing in the October 1978 issue of *Alternative Ulster*, Claire Dobson complained that the band was trading in "sensationalist ideas I can see on the *News at Ten* any night or read in the *Daily Express* over breakfast."[45] A particularly sharp example of this attack can be found in comments by P. Checkoff (aka Dave Hyndman), a member of Belfast's Anarchist Collective and co-owner of the Print Workshop: "They never attempted to tackle any real issues in the North, whilst being heralded as the representatives of Northern Irish youth. Indeed, their highly ambiguous lyrics argued for a 'normality' under which they could progress as a rock band, that the only thing in the North was the fact that they hadn't anywhere to play."[46] The band had defenders in the English press, which sometimes did not help their cause back home. Peter Silverton, writing in the Oct. 1978 issue of *Sounds*, defended the band with the rather patronizing claim, "People in that war-torn hell-hole have more reason than most to shout about things."[47]

Speaking years later, Stuart Bailie observed, "It's rather boring to go into the dodgy aesthetics of SLF all the time, but their posturing and contrived words were hard to take."[48] Perhaps the most forceful critics of the band were The Undertones from Derry. Their feuds became so notorious, Bailie characterized the two bands as "the oil and water of Ulster punk."[49] Yet, the Undertones' legitimate criticisms were frequently overshadowed by snide complaints driven by petty jealousy and sour grapes. In the press, members of The Undertones attacked the Stiffs for a wide range of supposed sins, both musical and lyrical.[50] Bassist Michael Bradley recalls, "There was definitely some animosity, based on nothing more than us thinking it was a crap idea to play up the Troubles angle. It was embarrassing when The Clash did it as well. Also the fact that the words from some of their songs came from a journalist didn't endear the whole thing to us either."[51] Lead singer Feargal Sharkey would later observe, "People used to ask early on why we didn't write songs about the Troubles; we were doing our best to escape from it."[52] The Undertones would go on to write the vindictive "Whizz Kids," off their 1980 *Hypnotised* album, about the Stiff Little Fingers.

Though they largely resisted joining the mudslinging, the Stiffs would often defend their decision to sing about the Troubles. In a 1980 *Melody Maker* interview, Jake stated, "I wasn't sensationalizing anything. In fact, I deliberately went out of my way not to; I was trying not to upset people there because some of the people who were killed were my friends, and I didn't want to upset their friends and family."[53] In an interview with *Sounds*, Jake was more direct: "Kids would say, 'You're only doing it to make money, you're cashing in on what you've been through.' It took somebody like Gordon who was an outsider to say, 'Fuck it. You're not exploiting anybody. You've been through it as well. Write about it if you believe in it.' So we did."[54] Both Jake and Henry have repeatedly claimed that only a handful of songs on *Inflammable Material* actually related to Belfast and the Troubles (nine of the thirteen by my count).[55]

Speaking of many Belfast punks' suspicions of the Stiffs, Brian Young observed that at some point "the penny finally dropped that Ogilvie's master plan might actually bear fruit, to our dismay and undying disgust . . . In hindsight I do think Ogilvie had cleverly targeted the exact audience he was after, the influential slightly older, concerned, Rough Trade hippy punk, guilt-ridden white middleclass people who were following the accepted trendy lefty party line on Northern Ireland. SLF were their perfect poster boys, until they found out that SLF weren't Republicans and didn't actually follow the tired old 'troops out' angle they all espoused from the safety of their cosy Hampstead homes. That angle certainly helped break SLF with the media. Personally I think it did the band a *huge* disservice, but hey it worked, so who am

I to argue!"[56] In hindsight, Henry has noted, "As we started doing our own stuff we got flak for sensationalizing the situation, and maybe with some justification. What we will never apologise for is that we did that—get noticed—and we certainly believed in what we played."[57]

But once they gained widespread attention for being a Belfast punk band singing about the Troubles, the Stiffs purposefully turned away—both lyrically and physically—from Belfast. And, as if proving the charge of being bandwagon jumpers, they slowly began shifting away from punk as well.

Evolving into a Mainstream Rock Band

A month after the release of *Inflammable Material*, the Stiff Little Fingers were back in the studio to record a new single, their first with Jim Reilly on drums. Released on May 8, 1978, "Gotta Gettaway" struck some as the band's justification for escaping the violence of Northern Ireland. In fact, it was an older song Jake had written about wanting to quit his mindless accounting job, similar to "Breakout" off *Inflammable Material*. While the band's first two singles had peaked in the Top 20 of the UK charts, "Gotta Gettaway" stalled at #38. Expectations on the band were exceedingly high. As Jake recalls, "the reviews [for *Inflammable Material*] were so outrageously over the top. It was almost a case of, 'How do we live up to this?' The *NME* was calling us the greatest rock'n'roll band in the world and we were thinking, 'We've only made one bloody record, this doesn't make sense.' None of it made sense to us. It was very flattering but we really were, 'How the hell do we live up to this?' And, of course, the other worry is how the fuck do we follow it?"[58]

The weight of external expectations partially informed the sophomore album, titled *Nobody's Heroes*. Recorded between January and February 1980, the album was released on March 7, 1980, and hit #8 on the UK album charts. But the Stiffs were no longer indie darlings, having released this follow-up on a major label. Despite what they sang in "Rough Trade," the band had been shopping for a major label deal as soon as *Inflammable Material* was released. It was readily apparent they had worked with Rough Trade primarily for convenience and not for any principled position. As Jake told *Hot Press* in January 1980, he "didn't want the band to become a martyr to the independent record business."[59]

Having proved their commercial viability with the success of *Inflammable Material*, the band signed a six-album deal with Chrysalis Records in August 1979. They received a £30,000 advance, which was significantly less than other offers, but came with a guarantee of complete artistic control. The contract also included a clause that the band would maintain copyright control and all licenses would revert to the band after seven years. As attractive as the offer was, it would never be as lucrative as the 50/50 royalty rate they had with Rough Trade. In defending their decision to leave Rough Trade, they noted the label's limited distribution network. In fact, at the time, Rough Trade had no distribution in the United States. American fans could only buy *Inflammable Material* as an expensive import.

To address the limited availability of *Inflammable Material* in some markets, the band decided to record and release a live album featuring songs from the first two albums. Chrysalis released the live recording of the band's July 20, 1980, show as *Hanx!* The album reached #9 on the UK charts, an impressive feat for a live album. Ironically, Rough Trade began distribution of *Inflammable Material* in the US around the time *Hanx!* was released. There seemed to be no ill will between the band and Rough Trade until several years later, when the label's rights timed out and the band opted to go with EMI for a CD reissue. Geoff Travis noted, "No one ever said to Mayo and I, 'Well you know what guys, you produced the record so let's sort out a producer contract.' That didn't happen. That's not particularly being treated right. We never got paid for it. We never got any royalties, never earned a cent out of it. We just did it out of love."[60] As an interesting aside, on the EMI CD release, Jim Reilly is listed as the band's drummer and there is no mention or credit given to Brian Faloon anywhere in the packaging.[61]

While *Nobody's Heroes* and *Hanx!* both charted, neither album enjoyed the same critical acclaim as the debut. Henry has argued the band's subsequent albums suffered from the impossibly high expectations created by *Inflammable Material*: "Basically those reviews [of later albums] highlighted how . . . over the top the reviews for the first album had been. From then on *Inflammable Material* started to become like a millstone round our necks."[62] While this was undoubtedly true, it is equally true that the band's sound was evolving away from punk and toward what their band biographer characterized as "guitar-driven hard-pop"[63] but could equally be classified as "mainstream rock." While their third studio album *Go for It* (released on April 17, 1981) managed to peak at #14 on the charts, the commercial appeal and critical respect of the band appeared to be on the decline.

At the end of 1981, Jim decided to leave the band due to frustrations with the band's musical direction. He stated, "I told them the new songs were shit musically and that the fans wouldn't like them. I've always considered myself a punk rock drummer and to me those songs sounded like Graham Parker and Elvis Costello, real lightweight pop . . . I told them straight I didn't want anything to do with it and that I was leaving."[64] The band replaced Reilly with Brian "Dolphin" Taylor, an English drummer from Middlesex. Henry has repeatedly stated that Jim's departure marked the decline of the band for him: "When Jim left, the Stiff Little Fingers ended. Anything since has been a weak version."[65] Elsewhere, he has noted, "That was the beginning of the end for me, the music then got softer . . . It always seemed more about money."[66]

In 1982, the Stiffs released *Now Then . . .*, what would be their final album for Chrysalis. The album featured several songs with horn sections, an acoustic ballad, and a cover of "Love of the Common People," a song Paul Young would have a global hit with the following year. With a few exceptions, most of the material on the album was rather flaccid, reflecting the band's embrace of mainstream pop-rock and a rejection of their punk roots. As Jake observed in a 1982 *Hot Press* interview to promote the album, "How do I justify Stiff Little Fingers to myself? I can't; I don't really. It seems very much like a memory at the moment. It's weird looking back on it because we don't play any track but one off the first album and that's 'Johnny Was,' the one we didn't write. We're making really conscious efforts to get away from it because we don't see it as relevant anymore."[67] Though the album hit #24 on the UK charts, it did not result in the mainstream commercial success the band, or at least some members, seemed to be striving for.

Internal hostilities continued to grow, and the band decided to call it quits, concluding a farewell tour in Glasgow on Sunday, February 6, 1983. However, this would not be the Stiff Little Fingers' final show. They reunited for what was intended to be a limited tour in December 1987. But after they were met with enthusiastic, often sold-out crowds, the band decided to reform permanently. They released an album of new material, *Flags and Emblems*, on Castle Records in 1991. But by that time, Ali had left the band and was replaced by bassist Bruce Foxton of The Jam. A few years later, they went into the studio to record their second post-reunion album, *Get a Life* (1994) also on Castle.

During these recordings, Jake fired Henry in circumstances and on grounds that remain contested. Jake claimed Henry hadn't bothered to learn the guitar parts to the new songs and spent the practice sessions playing Metallica riffs. He has quipped, "[Henry] wanted to be in a band. Just not this one."[68] Henry disputes this version, claiming, "I recorded my guitar parts for the *Get a Life* album and went home. Later I got a phone call from the manager Russell to say that the others had held a meeting and decided they didn't want me to be part of it anymore. At the time my so-called best friend of twenty years Jake Burns wouldn't speak to me. Whenever I phoned him, his wife would always say he was in the bath—for eight months!"[69] Elsewhere he has complained, "While they may have had their reasons it was cowardly the way it was done and the way they led people to believe I left of my own free will."[70] In a 2024 interview, Henry maintained that while Jake has never adequately explained the firing, there is no longer any animosity between the two, noting they are "friendly, but not close friends."[71]

Significantly, as the band's music evolved away from punk and their lyrical content stopped having anything to do with Northern Ireland, the Belfast punk scene it helped spawn entered its most vital and important era.

Taking Control of the Warzone:
Later Waves of Belfast Punk

By the early 1980s, the energy and revolutionary promise characterizing punk's global emergence seemed to have faded and calcified. Many of the first wave of bands—such as the Sex Pistols, Clash, the Damned, Ramones, Blondie, and Television—had either broken up or evolved into more mainstream bands, beginning the process that would see them join the pantheon of "Rock Bands" like the Stones and the Who, bands they had ostensibly been rebelling against. Of the Northern Irish bands associated with that initial burst of punk—Stiff Little Fingers, Rudi, Outcasts, Protex, Ruefrex, and the Undertones—many either signed to major record labels and/or tried their luck in England and beyond. Some of the Belfast punks grew out of the scene and settled into adult life, as had the original SLF drummer Brian Faloon. But another wave of punk emerged, grounded in the initial ethos of the first, but also decidedly different.

The Belfast scene had always benefited from its provincial status. As Roland Link observed, punk in Northern Ireland "remained largely indigenous from the grassroots level up and thus had time to develop and grow unhampered. Based on this solid foundation, punk rock in the Province developed into a strong, self-reliant, creative movement, which meant much more to the majority of its followers than just a short-lived rebellious fashion statement."[72] This became even truer in the 1980s as media and commercial interest in punk markedly dropped off. Petesy Burns, an active participant in Belfast punk for decades, claims the first wave of punk proved to be "prepubescent punk." He explains, "The sectarianism that was waiting to engulf the punks of '77/78 had to be dealt with in creative ways by the punks who came later. Between about '81 and '85 there were more punks, punk bands and punk gigs than there had ever been. This figure drastically increased between '86 and the early '90s."[73] Later punk bands of note included Runnin' Riot, Still Birth, Toxic Waste, Pink Turds in Space, and Stalag 17, to name a few. More importantly, outside the media spotlight, the Belfast scene evolved into something even more politically vital and relevant.[74]

After The Harp and other venues closed or stopped booking shows, the focal point of Belfast punk temporarily became the Anarchy Centre. The A-Centre, as it was affectionately known, briefly hosted all-age punk gigs, including the English anarcho-punk band Crass. Crass's dedication to both a DIY ethos of activism and anti-hierarchical anarchism greatly informed this second wave of Belfast punk. Later waves of punk in the 1980s and 1990s put many of the ideas of Belfast punk's first wave into practice and, by doing so, made a reality out of the promise of an "Alternative Ulster." The first non-sectarian punk community, centered around The Harp, Pound, and Good Vibrations, did not emerge by any great design, a point made by many of its participants. But when the A-Centre began organizing punk gigs a few years later, it *was* by design. And that was the same blueprint that then inspired the newly created Warzone Collective to institutionalize a communal space that wasn't just non-sectarian but *anti-sectarian*.[75] Formed in 1984, the Warzone Collective opened its first physical space two years later, providing a popular café/drop-in center, practice space, venue, recording studio, and screen-printing workshop. Sometimes referred to as the Warzone Centre, most people called it Giro's in honor of the unemployment benefit checks that sustained many users. As Kate Wimpress, one of the members of the collective, recalls, "Giro's was a cross-community space where you left the baggage that you might have grown up with very much at the door."[76] While The Harp had provided a safe space for punks to come together for pints and shows, the A-Centre and Giro's were places punks put theory into action.

It was there that later waves of Belfast punks worked to realize the promises of the early rhetoric of punk. As Chris Magee, another Warzone member noted, "Punk increasingly offered a space where questions could be asked about why society was divided and how those divisions could be overcome, offering a new politics entirely. The Warzone Centre allowed a space to develop where questions could be asked about the position of women in society, on issues of sexuality, on environmentalism and animal rights, and on the role of religion. It encouraged an environment and atmosphere where fanzines could be written and printed; bands could form, rehearse and perform; ideas could be discussed and debated; the like-minded could be encountered."[77] The space became an important countercultural hub for Belfast and the region.

Petesy Burns recalls, "Punk had always been a unifying factor but we wanted to go beyond that and create a space where people could truly work together and create something out of a seemingly hopeless situation."[78] Soon the rehearsal spaces were permanently booked, and the volunteers running the drop-in center had a hard time keeping up. Activist groups were using the place as a meeting space, and cultural events were packed, which forced them in 1991 to find a bigger space. Hilary Midgley, of the band Sledgehammer and a member of the Warzone Collective, recalls, "It was a center for people's freedom of expression on all levels—whether it was artistically or politically—and to just be able to sit in an environment with other people of like minds and create and develop that energy and that strength that we all had running through us. Certainly not before it and definitely not since has there been a group that has pulled people from all sides of the community in the way that it did."[79]

Since its emergence in the late 1970s, the Belfast punk scene had promoted political and cultural empowerment for a population that had been marginalized and terrorized for years. That process became more explicit in the 1980s and 1990s as punks like the Warzone Collective provided individuals with resources for participation and activism. For example, David Hyndman, who had earlier run the print shop over Hooley's Good Vibrations store, was part of the collective and worked with community groups to help them publish their complaints about housing and urban development. The Giro's café and drop-in center functioned as a space for discussing, organizing, and taking action. Zinester and collective activist Danny recalls that Warzone "was an inspiration and catalyst" for many: "Seeing and getting involved in all of it was indescribably positive especially against the background of sectarian war and the particularly ugly breeds of bastard nationalism we have here which had and continue to have absolutely fuck all to offer anyone anywhere!"[80] Stuart Martin, another active member of the scene, stated: "It's one thing talking about doing things and theorizing, but these were practical examples of real stuff—real exciting alternative stuff happening."[81]

While the first wave of punks in Belfast got the media attention, the following scenes arguably accomplished much more. As Rudi's Brian Young observed, "You can't overemphasize the importance of the Anarchy Centre, Just Books, and the Warzone Collective for making a positive impact in Belfast. The punk scene after Good Vibrations did more good work on the ground than Good Vibrations ever did. That isn't to slag off Good Vibrations. But they were more engaged. They had greater purpose and focus. None of those bands were on TV, *Top of the Pops*, but they did so much good work on the ground."[82]

An oft-repeated observation (occasionally credited to Terri Hooley) is that "punk was more popular in the north of Ireland than anywhere else in the world because we needed it more." In the 1970s, Stiff Little Fingers and their fellow punks disrupted the status quo with their pledge of taking "no more of that" and railing against the "wasted lives" lost to sectarian strife. By the 1980s and 1990s, punks were realizing the "Alternative Ulster" dream through DIY activism. As Petesy Burns recalls about the work of the Warzone Collective, "The message was simple: if you want to control what you create, you gotta do it yourself and not wait for someone to do it for you."[83] Thus, while politicians debated and negotiated about how to stop the violence, Belfast punks were helping to build the peace from the ground up.

6
Punkwashing
The Legacy of SLF and Punk in Belfast

In the summer of 2024, I joined several thousand people in the Custom House Square in the center of Belfast to watch Stiff Little Fingers take the stage. They headlined an event also featuring The Damned, Skids, and Terri Hooley performing DJ duties. The Stiffs have performed as part of the "Putting the Fast in Belfast" series for the past several years. That year marked the forty-fifth anniversary of the release of *Inflammable Material*. And while the band on stage was different than the one that recorded that stunning debut album, so too was Belfast.

On April 10, 1998—Good Friday—numerous representatives signed a pair of agreements that brought an end to most of the violence characterizing the Troubles. One treaty, the British-Irish Agreement signed between the governments of Britain and the Republic of Ireland, was intended to create the larger context by which peace could be maintained in Northern Ireland, which would be achieved through the other document, known as the Multi-Party Agreement. This latter agreement was signed by eight

Northern Irish political parties and entities, including three Unionist groups (Ulster Unionist Party, Progressive Unionist Party [linked to the UVF], and Ulster Democratic Party [of the UDF], two nationalist parties (Sinn Féin [linked to the IRA] and Social Democratic and Labour Party), and three independent groups (Alliance Party, Northern Ireland Women's Coalition, and the Labour Coalition). Collectively, these two treaties are known as the Belfast Agreement (or, more commonly, the Good Friday Agreement). They provide the foundation upon which a tenuous peace rests.

Scholars and policymakers make an important distinction between peacekeeping and peacebuilding. The former keeps combatants apart, usually by sending in a third party to act as a buffer, while the latter term refers to the process of addressing the root causes of the conflict and creating new ways of thinking and acting, upon which a sustainable peace can be established. The usual markers of achieving peace—things such as ceasefire announcements and the signing of peace deals, such as the Good Friday Agreement—are produced by politicians and generals, but the slow process of peacebuilding is often intangible and conducted at the grassroots level. Building peace usually entails average people actively defying the violent social divisions of their everyday life and forging alternative visions of the future. In Belfast and Northern Ireland, punks helped to lead the way. The punk scenes created important non-sectarian spaces in which social networks were built, alternative ways of being were imagined, and campaigns of political and social activism were realized, helping make the peace process a reality.

Stuart Bailie, journalist and author of *Trouble Songs: Music and Conflict in Northern Ireland*, argued, "I absolutely believe that punk rock helped to provoke the peace process. [By 1998], the vision of Alternative Ulster had become self-realizing."[1] But it wasn't exactly self-realizing. It took a great deal of time and energy from many committed individuals. Bailie knows this well, playing an instrumental role in creating and sustaining Belfast's Oh Yeah! Centre, which continues to be a cultural hub, providing invaluable resources for Belfast musicians today. The role of punks in helping transform life in Northern Ireland to the degree that an "Alternative Ulster" became realizable should not be dismissed. In fact, in 2019, I walked into the Ulster Museum in Belfast, Northern Ireland to visit their acclaimed exhibition on the Troubles. Entering the multi-room exhibit, with its almost four decades of Troubles-related artifacts, I could not help but notice the mannequin displayed in the center of the first room, as if occupying the pride of place. It was dressed in a spiked, black leather jacket with "OUTCASTS" hand-painted on the back. It was the jacket of Greg Cowan of The Outcasts. The museum curators clearly understood Northern Ireland's punk scenes were both a significant product of and a response to the crippling violence characterizing everyday life for the population, especially the youth. But the inclusion of Cowan's jacket also hinted to another phenomenon: the mythologizing of punk's history in Belfast. For several years now, memorializing punk has been used to promote cultural tourism to the city. Or, to coin a phrase, "punkwashing." And a significant element in this process has been the Stiff Little Fingers.

Punk Nostalgia, Cultural Tourism, and Political Change

The city center on the weekend of the concert was awash with ageing punks sporting various SLF T-shirts. Both the Waterboys and Liam Gallagher of Oasis were also playing in Belfast that weekend, but their fans seemed few and far between. Rather, the city center was so overrun by punks it would have boggled the mind back in 1977. Of course, the city center of 2024 was now a markedly different place.

Sections of the city remain segregated. When walking through the loyalist neighborhood of Sandy Row, for example, the weight of history is apparent. Unionist sentiment is still very much explicit throughout the neighborhood. Loyalist flags and murals decorate buildings, alongside the occasional pro-UDA graffiti. The Sandy Row neighborhood abuts the Catholic-dominated Falls Road neighborhood, itself festooned with republican symbols, murals, and memorials. The two neighborhoods continue to be separated by so-called "peace walls," still in place decades after the signing of the Good Friday Agreement. With so many continuing markers of sectarianism, the peace seems precarious.

Yet, these pockets of sectarianism also seem anachronistic. For many, it is hard to imagine a return to the violence of the Troubles. The city center vibrates with cosmopolitan energy. Tourists weave through the sidewalks. Every evening, packs of young teenage boys with matching haircuts laugh about, while groups of fashionably dressed young women head out for the night. Bachelor and bachelorette parties abound. "Party buses" seem to clog traffic on every other street, propelled by boisterous pedaling drinkers. Today's

Belfast city center is a far cry from the desolate no-go zone surrounded by cement barricades and barbed wire.

Demographically, Northern Ireland is definitely changing. In the 2001 census, the number of Protestants dropped below 50 percent for the first time in history, though they still slightly outnumbered Catholics. That changed with the 2021 census when the number of Catholics by background (45.7 percent) surpassed the number of Protestant and other Christian groups by background (43.48 percent), representing the plurality, with no group in the overall majority.[2] What these changes mean for the future of Northern Ireland remains an open question.

As much as Belfast is a different city, Stiff Little Fingers are a different band. After Jake fired Henry during the recording of 1994's *Get a Life*, Jake continued to record and tour under the Stiff Little Fingers name, releasing several albums, including *Tinderbox* (1997, Abstract), *Hope Street* (1999, Oxygen), *Guitar and Drum* (2003, Kung Fu Records) and *No Going Back* (2014, Rigid Digits). For most of those albums, Jake was the only original member left in the band. Ali McMordie eventually returned to bass duties in 2006.

When they took the stage that Saturday night in August 2024, the band featured only two members—Jake and Ali—who had played on *Inflammable Material*. The other two musicians on stage were guitarist Ian McCallum and drummer Steve Grantley. Though neither had played on the band's first four albums, both have been in the band since the 1990s.

In what could have been regarded as a provocative move, but was probably simply a smart financial decision, a band called XSLF played in Belfast the night before the Stiffs big show. The cheekily named XSLF was formed in 2013 by former members Henry Cluney and Jim Reilly. In addition to material off their two studio albums, *Arrup Bang* (2017) and *Northstar* (2019), their live sets draw heavily from the first three SLF albums. After Jim Reilly retired, Henry Cluney continued with XSLF. For that August show, XSLF played to a capacity crowd at a small venue a few blocks from the site of the original Harp. Yet, their crowd seemed miniscule compared to the thousands attending the Custom House Square show the next night. Unsurprisingly, both bands played similar sets that weekend, drawing heavily from *Inflammable Material* and *Nobody's Heroes*. And to underscore the fact that the punk scene in Belfast remains vibrant and vital to this day, as the Stiffs were indulging in a bit a nostalgia in Custom House Square, five contemporary punk bands ripped up the stage at the Oh Yeah! Centre a few blocks away.

Punkwashing

As Belfast continues to grapple with the deep wounds and unresolved tensions of its past, as well as its uncertain post-Brexit future, the city began co-opting its punk legacy to promote cultural tourism. A plaque outside of the site of the old Harp pub commemorates the "Home of Belfast Punk Rock." The Stiff Little Fingers are listed on the plaque as one of the bands performing there in the late 1970s, despite having only played three times. A new Harp pub, close by but entirely unrecognizable from its namesake, stocks Punk IPA in its cooler. Around the corner, a high-end pizzeria markets the street cred of its "punk pizza." Several murals in the area depict Northern Irish musicians, including a few recognizable punk faces.

A plaque also hangs outside the former site of the Trident bar in Bangor, immortalized in the lyrics of "Alternative Ulster." The plaque proclaims the site to be the birthplace of punk in Northern Ireland. While the plaque outside of the former Harp is a state-sanctioned memorial, the Trident plaque is an unofficial act attributed to the "Alternative Ulster Historical Society."[3]

Back in Belfast, the building on Great Victoria Street that once housed Good Vibrations is now a public art installation, covered in a celebratory graffiti mural, including a two-storied high portrait of the admittedly larger-than-life Terri Hooley. Interestingly, at the top of the building, the mural is centered by "Stiff Little Fingers" and their flame logo from the cover of *Inflammable Material,* with "Alternative Ulster" stenciled across the front in huge letters. Again, the Stiffs were never on the Good Vibrations label. In fact, Hooley was rather dismissive of the band, frequently quipping: "They're not even in my Top 5000 favourite bands."[4] Yet, the Stiffs are the only band name commemorated on the building. Throughout Belfast, there are several other government-sponsored murals that feature members of punk's first wave. Punk is now being celebrated in a city where punks were treated violently decades before.

Hooley himself has been made the subject of not only a feature film but a musical theatrical production, both entitled *Good Vibrations* (and definitely worth checking out). He is now a celebrated figure in a city in which he faced harassment and physical intimidation from virtually every side of the conflict for years. And then there is the leather jacket in the middle of the Ulster Museum, from a band whose members were so vilified and ostracized at the time they named themselves "The Outcasts."

In modern Belfast, the city's punk legacy has been sanitized and co-opted for cultural tourism. After John Peel's death in 2004, somebody graffitied lyrics from The Undertones' hit song "Teenage Kicks" on the Bridge End flyover in East Belfast. The graffiti was redesigned and is now maintained by the city, painted by local youths from the South Strand and lower Newtonards Road areas, under the aegis of the East Belfast Partnership.[5] Recall that The Undertones hailed from Derry, not Belfast. Yet, the city has worked purposefully to capitalize on punk's heritage and impact on the city. Many former participants of the Belfast punk scenes lament what some call the "Disneyfication" of Belfast punk's history, glossing over and buffing out inconvenient truths and contradictions. Others point out how this nostalgia erases the important political work that later punks associated with Giro's and the Warzone Collective achieved. There are no plaques commemorating the Warzone and the site of its last location was recently demolished and replaced with an office building. Perhaps it is more palatable to praise Hooley's entrepreneurship than the Warzone's anarchist sensibilities.

And don't forget the annual punk concert, complete with corporate sponsorship, held in the heart of the city and featuring the Stiff Little Fingers—a band Belfast now proudly claims as their own despite the band relocating to London before their debut album was even released.

Yet, it is undeniable that the band and their songs are as popular in Belfast today as they ever were. That weekend, SLF (and XSLF) received their warmest responses when they played the songs from *Inflammable Material* that spoke directly to the Troubles: "Suspect Device," "Wasted Life," "Johnny Was," and, of course, "Alternative Ulster." Yet, as Jake wryly observed, "The fact that the [band's] Northern Irish songs are still relevant today is a sad indictment of Northern Ireland."[6]

At the very least, the current celebration of the band as hometown heroes is just another chapter in the complicated relationship between the city, the band, and the punk scene it emerged from. For all their faults and complications, the Stiffs remain an important part of Belfast, its people, and its history. Ultimately, I agree with Stuart Bailie, who argued, "I believe that if you trace the start of the French Revolution back to some rather insolent plays by Marivaux, then it follows that the peace process in Northern Ireland was founded on the opening chords of 'Suspect Device.'"[7]

Setting aside all the punkwashing and corporate-sponsored punk nostalgia, it is worth remembering that punk made a difference in Belfast. For many, it wasn't just a fashion statement or a trend, but a vehicle with which to alter their social reality. Not just to articulate a non-sectarian stance through song, but to actively practice anti-sectarianism within a community of like-minded people. It provided the resources to imagine an "Alternative Ulster" and make it a reality.

Standing in the middle of Custom House Square, singing the lyrics to "Suspect Device," "Wasted Life," and "Alternative Ulster" with Jake Burns and thousands of other fans, was an undeniably powerful and moving experience. It drove home the point that even though music cannot change the world—because music has no agency of its own—it can inspire people to believe *their* actions can make a difference in the world. And in Belfast, it did just that.

Notes

Preface

1 Paul Morley, "Review of Stiff Little Fingers' *Inflammable Material*," *New Musical Express*. February 10, 1979.

2 Roland Link, *Kicking Up A Racket: The Story of Stiff Little Fingers 1977–1983* (Appletree, 2009), 191.

3 When EMI re-released the album on CD in 2001, they changed the color of the flame icons to match the red of the band and album's name.

4 Stuart Bailie, *Trouble Songs: Music and Conflict in Northern Ireland* (Bloomfield Press, 2018), 9.

5 Kevin C. Dunn, *Global Punk: Resistance and Rebellion in Everyday Life* (Bloomsbury Academic, 2016).

6 Matt Davies, "Do It Yourself: Punk Rock and the Disalienation of International Relations," in *Resounding International Relations: On Music, Culture, and Politics*, ed. Marianne Franklin (Palgrave, 2005), 126.

7 Brian Young, interview with author, March 5, 2019.

8 Peter Dale, *Anyone Can Do It: Empowerment, Tradition and the Punk Underground* (Ashgate, 2012).

9 Quoted in Sean O'Neil and Guy Trelford, *It Makes You Want to Spit!: The Definitive Guide to Punk in Northern Ireland 1977–1982* (Reekus Music, 2003), 262.

10 Dick Hebdige, *Subculture: The Meaning of Style* (Routledge,1979), 90.

11 Francis Stewart, "Alternative Ulster: Punk Rock as a Means of Overcoming Religious Divide in Northern Ireland," in *Irish Religious Conflict in Comparative Perspective*, ed. John Wolffe (Palgrave Macmillan, 2014).

12 Lawrence Grossberg, *We Gotta Get Out of This Place: Popular Conservatism and Post Modern Culture* (Routledge, 1992).

Chapter 1

1 A few points on terminology. England is a country occupying the southern part of the British Isles. Great Britain refers to all three countries located on the British Isles: England, Scotland, and Wales. The United Kingdom is the sovereign political entity composed of those three countries, as well as Northern Ireland. The British Empire includes Britain as well as the numerous colonial holdings it acquired over time, peaking during the nineteenth -twentieth centuries.

2 There are numerous works on general Irish history, but a particularly useful one remains T. W. Moody and F. X. Martin's edited work *The Course of Irish History*, 5th edition (Rinehart, 2012).

3 Julian Moynahan, *Anglo-Irish: The Literary Imagination in a Hyphenated Culture* (Princeton University Press, 1995).

4   James Anderson and Ian Shuttleworth, "Sectarian Demography, Territoriality and Political Development in Northern Ireland," *Political Geography* 17, no. 2 (1998): 187–208.

5   Tim Pat Coogan, *The IRA: Fully revised and updated* (Palgrave, 2000), 332–8.

6   In addition to obvious examples of employment discrimination, this movement gained traction by also focusing on systemic housing discrimination. For example, between 1945–67, the government built 1,048 houses, but only 195 went to Catholic families.

7   There are numerous books on The Troubles, but a particularly useful one is Tim Pat Coogan's *The Troubles: Ireland's Ordeal and the Search for Peace* (Palgrave, 2002).

8   Chris Ryder, *The RUC, 1922–1997: A Force under Fire*, 3rd rev. edition (Random House, 1997).

9   Another point of terminology. Originally called Derry (Doire in Gaelic), the city's name was officially changed to Londonderry in 1612 during the creation of the Ulster Plantation. Historically, Catholic/nationalist residents have continued referring to it as Derry, while Protestant/unionists (and their British compatriots) tended to employ its official name. In 1984, the city council voted to change the city's name back to Derry, a move not legally recognized by the British courts. This text will use "Derry" as that is the most common usage by its residents today.

10 Kevin Myers, *Watching the Door: Cheating Death in 1970s Belfast* (Atlantic Books, 2008), 96.

11 Greil Marcus, *Lipstick Traces: A Secret History of the Twentieth Century* (Harvard University Press, 1989), 64.

12 Petesy Burns, interview with author, February 6, 2019.

13 Greg Cowan, interview with author. April 2, 2019.

Chapter 2

1 Link, *Kicking Up A Racket*, 24.

2 Jake Burns and Alan Parker, *Stiff Little Fingers: Song by Song* (Sanctuary Publishing, 2003), 9.

3 Burns and Parker, *Still Little Fingers*, 15.

4 Quoted in Link, *Kicking Up a Racket*, 25.

5 Burns and Parker, *Still Little Fingers*, 15.

6 Link, *Kicking Up a Racket*, 26.

7 Ibid.

8 Ibid.

9 Ibid., 28–9.

10 Ibid., 29.

11 Henry Cluney, interview with author, August 7, 2024.

12 Quoted in Link, *Kicking Up a Racket*, 29.

13 Cluney, interview with author.

14 Quoted in Link, *Kicking Up a Racket*, 31.

15 Cluney, interview with author.

16 Burns and Parker, *Still Little Fingers*, 21.

17 Cluney, interview with author.

18 Jake Burns, interview with Alan Parker, bonus track on *Inflammable Material* CD (EMI, 2001).

19 Cluney, interview with author.

20 Quoted in Link, *Kicking Up a Racket*, 38.

21 Cluney, interview with author.

22 Link, *Kicking Up a Racket*, 39–40.

23 Quoted in Link, *Kicking Up a Racket*, 41.

24 Burns and Parker, *Still Little Fingers*, 23–4.

25 Burns, CD interview with Alan Parker.

26 Quoted in Bailie, *Trouble Songs*, 130.

27 Quoted in Link, *Kicking Up a Racket*, 42.

28 Ibid.

29 Ibid., 43.

30 Ibid., 46.

31 Quoted in Bailie, *Trouble Songs*, 129.

32 Link, *Kicking Up a Racket*, 49.

33 Burns and Parker, *Still Little Fingers*, 26.

34 Quoted in Link, *Kicking Up a Racket*, 52.

35 Ibid., 53.

36 Cowan, interview with author.

37 O'Neil and Trelford, *It Makes You Want to Spit!*, 46–7.

38 Quoted in Bailie, *Trouble Songs*, 104.

39 Ibid., 102–3.

40 Martin McLoone, "Punk Music in Northern Ireland," *Irish Studies Review* 12, no. 1 (2004): 29.

41 Bailie, *Trouble Songs*, 108–9. Young and Cowan, interviews with the author.

42 Quoted in Link, *Kicking Up a Racket*, 69.

43 Ibid., 53.

44 Ibid., 56.

45 Ibid., 58.

46 Ibid., 59.

47 Ibid., 60.

48 Burns and Parker, *Still Little Fingers*, 33.

Chapter 3

1 Quoted in Link, *Kicking Up a Racket*, 63–4.

2 Coogan, *The IRA*.

3 Eamonn Mallie and Patrick Bishop, *The Provisional IRA* (Heinemann, 1987).

4 Quoted in Bailie, *Trouble Songs*, 133.

5 Link, *Kicking Up a Racket*, 64. While the plagiarism is obvious, Burns admitted to plundering the song (which was co-written by Hagar) in a March 1980 *NME* interview. See also Mick Middles, "Stiff Little Fingers: The Voice Squad," *Sounds*, March 1, 1980.

6 Bailie, *Trouble Songs*, 133.

7 Burns and Parker, *Still Little Fingers*, 38.

8 Quoted in Burns and Parker, *Still Little Fingers*, 38.

9 Quoted in Link, *Kicking Up a Racket*, 79.

10 Ibid., 83.

11 Tony Stewart, "It's a Dog's Life in Today's Belfast," *New Musical Express*. March 25, 1978, 11.

12 Quoted in Link, *Kicking Up a Racket*, 81.

13 Link, *Kicking Up a Racket*, 78.

14 Stewart, "It's a Dog's Life," 11.

15 Quoted in Bailie, *Trouble Songs*, 135–6.

16 Ibid., 136.

17 Quoted in Burns and Parker, *Still Little Fingers*, 39. In a 2002 interview with *Mojo*, Jake continued to claim that at least one record company employee "threw it in a bucket of water." Quoted in Link, *Kicking Up a Racket*, 82.

18 Quoted in Link, *Kicking Up a Racket*, 85.

19 Quoted in Burns and Parker, *Still Little Fingers*, 40. Also Link, *Kicking Up a Racket*, 85, and Burns, CD interview with Alan Parker.

20 Link, *Kicking Up a Racket*, 160.

21 Ulster TV, "It Makes You Want To Spit," Documentary, 1978. Available at https://youtu.be/mnPmE-q4jS8?si =luJCAxEe8HsvUEhl. Accessed October 3, 2024.

22 Burns and Parker, *Still Little Fingers*, 30.

23 Cowan, interview with author.

24 Link, *Kicking Up a Racket*, 117.

25 Young, interview with author.

26 Quoted in Link, *Kicking Up a Racket*, 117.

27 Burns and Parker, *Still Little Fingers*, 29.

28 Quoted in O'Neil and Trelford, *It Makes You Want to Spit!*, 263.

29 Stewart, "It's a Dog's Life," 11.

30 O'Neil and Trelford, *It Makes You Want to Spit!*, 20.

31 Burns and Parker, *Still Little Fingers*, 45–6; Link, *Kicking Up a Racket*, 87.

32 Hollis is sometimes mistakenly assumed to be the "Eddie" in the band's name, but no such person existed, except for a dummy they used for early gigs and then ditched after the joke got old.

33 Burns, CD interview with Alan Parker.

34 Quoted in Link, *Kicking Up a Racket*, 101.

35 Ibid.

36 Burns and Parker, *Still Little Fingers*, 45.

37 Quoted in Link, *Kicking Up a Racket*, 112.

38 Ibid., 113.

39 Not only did TRB not require the Stiffs to pay to join the tour, as was the practice at the day, they actually paid the band to be the opener. As Jake would later recall, this was "astonishingly generous" of them, quoted in Burns' CD interview with Alan Parker.

40 Quoted in Bailie, *Trouble Songs*, 138.

41 Quoted in Link, *Kicking Up a Racket*, 125.

42 Bailie, *Trouble Songs*, 8.

43 Link, *Kicking Up a Racket*, 87.

44 Bailie, *Trouble Songs*, 8–9.

45 Quoted in Link, *Kicking Up a Racket*, 87.

46 Matthew Collin, "Belfast: The War against Cliché," *The Guardian*, January 23, 2003.

47 Burns and Parker, *Still Little Fingers*, 49.

48 Link, *Kicking Up a Racket*, 100.

49 Quoted in Link, *Kicking Up a Racket,* 133.

50 Ibid., 134.

51 Ibid.

52 Cluney, interview with author.

53 Burns and Parker, *Still Little Fingers,* 58–9.

54 Link, *Kicking Up a Racket,* 130–1.

55 Ibid., 132.

Chapter 4

1 Burns and Parker, *Still Little Fingers,* 23–4.

2 Fionna McCann, "'Special Powers' in the North of Ireland: Abuse, Repression, and Resistance," *The Funambulist* #29 (April 2020): 50–3. Available at https: / /thefunambulist.net / magazine /states-of-emergency /special-powers-in-the-no rth-of-ireland-abuse-repression-and-resistance-by-fiona -mccann. Accessed September 4, 2024.

3 Cluney, interview with author.

4 Martin Melaugh, "Estimates of the Strength of Paramilitary Groups," Ulster University's CAIN [Conflict Archive on the Internet] Project. Available at https: / /cain.ulster.ac.uk /issues /violence /paramilitary2.htm. Accessed September 5, 2024.

5 Quoted in Link, *Kicking Up a Racket,* 146.

6 Burns and Parker, *Still Little Fingers,* 34–5.

7 Quoted in Link, *Kicking Up a Racket,* 64.

8 Link, *Kicking Up a Racket,* 64.

9 Burns and Parker, *Still Little Fingers,* 34.

10   Quoted in Bailie, *Trouble Songs*, 135.

11   Burns and Parker, *Still Little Fingers*, 35.

12   Ibid., 50.

13   Link, *Kicking Up a Racket*, 87.

14   Cluney, interview with author.

15   Burns and Parker, *Still Little Fingers*, 50–1.

16   Quoted in Bailie, *Trouble Songs*, 141.

17   Burns and Parker, *Still Little Fingers*, 51.

18   Link, *Kicking Up a Racket*, 80.

19   Quoted in Link, *Kicking Up a Racket*, 81.

20   Daniel Rachel, *Walls Come Tumbling Down: Rock Against Racism, 2 Tone, Red Wedge* (Picador, 2017), 159–60.

21   Link, *Kicking Up a Racket*, 95–6.

22   Ibid., 80.

23   Burns and Parker, *Still Little Fingers*, 51–2.

24   Ibid., 52–3.

25   Stewart, "It's a Dog's Life," 11.

26   Ronald Weitzer, *Policing Under Fire: Ethnic Conflict and Police-Community Relations in Northern Ireland* (SUNY Press, 1995).

27   Burns and Parker, *Still Little Fingers*, 52.

28   Quoted in Link, *Kicking Up a Racket*, 104.

29   Burns and Parker, *Still Little Fingers*, 53–4.

30   Statista, "Total Number of Deaths per Year during the Troubles (the Northern Ireland Conflict) from 1969 to 2001." Available at: https: / /www.statista.com /statistics /1401907 / ni-troubles-deaths-annual /. Accessed September 15, 2024.

31 Burns and Parker, *Still Little Fingers*, 54–5.

32 Ibid., 55.

33 Ibid., 49.

34 Cluney, interview with author.

Chapter 5

1   Gary Bushell, "Review of Stiff Little Fingers' *Inflammable Material*," *Sounds*, February 10, 1979.

2   Morley, "Review of *Inflammable Material*."

3   Quoted in Link, *Kicking Up a Racket*, 151.

4   Link, *Kicking Up a Racket*, 154.

5   Ibid., 136–9.

6   Quoted in Link, *Kicking Up a Racket*, 169.

7   Ibid., 158.

8   Link, *Kicking Up a Racket*, 157.

9   Quoted in Link, *Kicking Up a Racket*, 153.

10 Ibid., 146.

11 John T. Davis, "Shellshock Rock," Documentary. Released 1979. Available at https://youtu.be/W07YLWeSOI4?si =13PfHBtVjiYlVt43. Accessed March 3, 2019.

12 McLoone, "Punk Music in Northern Ireland," 35.

13 Gavin Martin, "Northern Ireland: The Fantasy and The Reality," *New Musical Express*, October 11, 1980, 34.

14 Link, *Kicking Up a Racket*, 99.

15 Brian Young, correspondence with author, December 30, 2024.

16 Ricky Adam, *Belfast Punk: Warzone Collective 1997–2003.* (Damiani, 2017), 170.

17 Bailie, *Trouble Songs*, 11.

18 John Street, *Rebel Rock: The Politics of Popular Music* (Basil Blackwell, 1986), 3.

19 Young, interview with author.

20 O'Neil and Trelford, *It Makes You Want to Spit!*, 97.

21 Quoted in Bailie, *Trouble Songs*, 123.

22 Cowan, interview with author.

23 Quoted in Terri Hooley and Richard Sullivan, *Hooleygan: Music, Mayhem, Good Vibrations* (Blackstaff Press, 2010), 142.

24 O'Neil and Trelford, *It Makes You Want to Spit!*, 255. Brian Young recalls this gig as being by The Doomed (a version of The Damned) at the Pound.

25 Quoted in Stewart, "Alternative Ulster," 38.

26 O'Neil and Trelford, *It Makes You Want to Spit!*, 112.

27 Anna Burns, *Milkman* (Faber & Faber, 2018), 24–5.

28 Alberto Melucci, *Nomads of the Present: Social Movements and Individual Needs in Contemporary Society* (Temple University Press, 1989), 75.

29 As noted earlier, the song was written specifically in response to the Bedford Street Riots. The band would later drop the song from their set, aware that people who hadn't been there could be interpreting it as cheap sloganeering.

30 Link, *Kicking Up a Racket*, 96.

31 Cluney, Cowan, and Young: interviews with author.

32   Terri Hooley, interview with author. March 4, 2019.

33   Ibid.

34   Kevin C. Dunn, "How Punk Saved Belfast," *Razorcake*, 121 (April/May 2021): 34–43.

35   Quoted in Link, *Kicking Up a Racket*, 93.

36   Quoted in O'Neil and Trelford, *It Makes You Want to Spit!*, 224.

37   Paul Morley, "Belfast's Ripped Back Sides," *New Musical Express*, February 17, 1979.

38   Quoted in Link, *Kicking Up a Racket*, 67.

39   Dave McCullough (aka "D. Angry"), "LAMF," *Alternative Ulster* 72 (1978): 2.

40   Peter Silverton, "Stiff Little Fingers: profile and interview," *Sounds*, October 7, 1978.

41   Quoted in Link, *Kicking Up a Racket*, 100.

42   Cluney, interview with author. See also O'Neil and Trelford, *It Makes You Want to Spit!*, 206.

43   Davis, "Shellshock Rock."

44   P.J. Kinzer, "Northern Irish Punks Protex Get Ready for Their Nashville Debut," *Nashville Scene*, March 6, 2024. Available at https://www.nashvillescene.com/music/features/protex -aidan-murtagh-interview-northern-ireland-punk-eastside -bowl-nashville/article_6969,685,774-da83-11ee-934e -439df339bf24.html. Accessed September 30, 2024.

45   Claire Dobson, "SLF," *Alternative Ulster*, no. 8 (October 1978); also quoted in Link, *Kicking Up a Racket*, 123.

46   Quoted in O'Neil and Trelford, *It Makes You Want to Spit!*, 4.

47   Silverton, "Stiff Little Fingers."

48   Quoted in O'Neil and Trelford, *It Makes You Want to Spit!*, viii.

49   Bailie, *Trouble Songs*, 260.

50   For example, see Harry Doherty, "Puttin' on the anti-style," *Melody Maker*, March 10, 1979, 18.

51   Quoted in Link, *Kicking Up a Racket*, 88.

52   Quoted in Timothy A. Heron, "Alternative Ulster: How Punk Took on the Troubles," *Irish Times*, December 2, 2016. Available at http://irishtimes.com/culture/books/alternative -ulster-how punk-took-on-the-troubles-1.2890644. Accessed January 29, 2019.

53   Quoted in Link, *Kicking Up a Racket*, 89.

54   Ibid., 66.

55   Cluney, interview with author. See also O'Neil and Trelford, *It Makes You Want to Spit!*, 217.

56   Quoted in Link, *Kicking Up a Racket*, 118.

57   Ibid., 10.

58   Burns and Parker, *Still Little Fingers*, 58.

59   Quoted in Link, *Kicking Up a Racket*, 170.

60   Ibid., 172.

61   It seems this was a decision made exclusively by EMI. When I mentioned the omission to Henry and Jake seperately, they were both incredulous and outraged.

62   Quoted in Link, *Kicking Up a Racket*, 204.

63   Ibid., 240.

64   Ibid., 263.

65   Cluney, interview with author.

66 Quoted in O'Neil and Trelford, *It Makes You Want to Spit!*, 209, 217.

67 Quoted in Bill Graham, "Interview with Jake Burns of Stiff Little Fingers," *Hot Press*, 1982., Available at https://www.hotpress.com/music/happy-birthday-jake-burns-read-a-1982-interview-with-stiff-little-fingers-frontman-23009754. Accessed October 11, 2024.

68 Quoted in Link, *Kicking Up a Racket*, 323.

69 Ibid.

70 Quoted in O'Neil and Trelford, *It Makes You Want to Spit!*, 209, 211.

71 Cluney, interview with author.

72 Link, *Kicking Up a Racket*, 68.

73 Quoted in O'Neil and Trelford, *It Makes You Want to Spit!*, 209, 200.

74 Dunn, "How Punk Saved Belfast."

75 Jim Donaghey, "Punk in Belfast, Northern Ireland: Critical Perspectives on the Troubles and Post-conflict 'Peace,'" In *The Oxford Handbook of Punk Rock*, ed. George McKay and Gina Arnold (Oxford University Press, 2020).

76 Northern Visions NVTV, "Giro's," documentary. April 16, 2010. Available at https://vimeo.com/10976273. Accessed August 16, 2019.

77 Ibid.

78 Burns, interview with author.

79 Northern Visions NVTV, "Giro's," documentary. See also "Belfast Warzone Collective—1980s Northern Ireland Punk/Anarchist Scene." Available at https://youtu.be/MLzAc4Yz3yk?si=4U4VQ2Pf4JbBxaQr. Accessed October 3, 2024.

80 Xvx, Mittens, "The Story of the Warzone Collective," 2014. Available at https://diyconspiracy.net/the-warzone-collective/. Accessed September 5, 2019.

81 Northern Visions NVTV, "Giro's," documentary.

82 Young, interview with author.

83 Adam, *Belfast Punk*, 12.

Chapter 6

1 Stuart Bailie, interview with author, February 5, 2019. See also Stuart Bailie, "I Believe Punk Rock Helped the Peace Process," *Irish Times,* May 11, 2018. Available at https://www.irishtimes .com/culture/books/i-believe-punk-rock-helped-the-peace -process-1.3490689. Accessed January 29, 2019.

2 Megan Specia and Ed O'Loughlin, "Catholics Outnumber Protestants in Norther Ireland for the First Time," *The New York Times,* September 22, 2022).

3 Anne-Marie Foster, "Alternative Ulster: Marking punk's Bangor Birthplace," *BBC News,* September 10, 2018. Available at https://www.bbc.com/news/uk-northern-ireland-45317415. Accessed September 25, 2024. See also Fearghus Roulston, *Belfast Punk and The Troubles: An Oral History* (Manchester University Press, 2022), 54.

4 Hooley, interview with author. See also Link, *Kicking Up a Racket,* 99.

5   Helen Jones, "Teenage Kicks Mural Reinstated in Belfast after Outcry," *BBC News*, March 16, 2015. Available at https://www.bbc.com/news/uk-northern-ireland-31909136. Accessed September 15, 2024. See also Roulston, *Belfast Punk and The Troubles*, 54–5.

6   Burns and Parker, *Still Little Fingers*, 74.

7   Quoted in Link, *Kicking Up a Racket*, 8.

Bibliography

Adam, Ricky. *Belfast Punk: Warzone Collective 1997-2003*. Bologna: Damiani, 2017.

Anderson, James and Ian Shuttleworth. "Sectarian Demography, Territoriality and Political Development in Northern Ireland." *Political Geography* 17, no. 2 (1998): 187–208.

Bailie, Stuart. "I Believe Punk Rock Helped the Peace Process." *Irish Times,* May 11, 2018. Available at https://www.irishtimes .com/culture/books/i-believe-punk-rock-helped-the-peace -process-1.3490689. Accessed January 29, 2019.

Bailie, Stuart. *Trouble Songs: Music and Conflict in Northern Ireland*. Belfast: Bloomfield Press, 2018.

Bailie, Stuart, interview with author, February 5, 2019.

"Belfast Warzone Collective – 1980s Northern Ireland Punk/ Anarchist Scene." Documentary. Available at https://youtu.be/ MLzAc4Yz3yk?si=4U4VQ2Pf4JbBxaQr. Accessed October 3, 20204.

Burns, Anna. *Milkman*. London: Faber & Faber, 2018.

Burns, Jake and Alan Parker. *Stiff Little Fingers: Song by Song*. London: Sanctuary Publishing, 2003.

Burns, Petesy, interview with author, February 6, 2019.

Bushell, Gary. "Review of Stiff Little Fingers' Inflammable Material." *Sounds*, February 10, 1979.

Cluney, Henry, interview with author, August 7, 2024.

Collin, Matthew. "Belfast: The War Against Cliché." *The Guardian,* January 23, 2003.

Coogan, Tim Pat. *The IRA: Fully Revised and Updated.* New York: Palgrave, 2000.

Coogan, Tim Pat. *The Troubles: Ireland's Ordeal and the Search for Peace.* New York: Palgrave, 2002.

Cowan, Brian, interview with author, April 2, 2019.

Dale, Peter. *Anyone Can Do It: Empowerment, Tradition and the Punk Underground.* London: Ashgate, 2012.

Davies, Matt. "Do It Yourself: Punk Rock and the Disalienation of International Relations." In *Resounding International Relations: On Music, Culture, and Politics,* edited by Marianne Franklin. New York: Palgrave, 2005.

Davis, John T. "Shellshock Rock." Documentary. Released 1979. Available at https://youtu.be/W07YLWeSOI4?si =13PfHBtVjiYlVt43. Accessed March 3, 2019.

Dobson, Claire. "SLF." *Alternative Ulster,* no. 8, October 1978.

Doherty, Harry. "Puttin' on the Anti-style." *Melody Maker,* March 10, 1979, 17–18, 47.

Donaghey, Jim. "Punk in Belfast, Northern Ireland: Critical Perspectives on the Troubles and Post-conflict 'Peace.'" In *The Oxford Handbook of Punk Rock,* edited by George McKay and Gina Arnold. Oxford: Oxford University Press, 2020.

Dunn, Kevin. *Global Punk: Resistance and Rebellion in Everyday Life.* London: Bloomsbury Academic, 2016.

Dunn, Kevin. "How Punk Saved Belfast." *Razorcake* 121 (April/ May 2021): 34–43.

Foster, Ann-Marie. "Alternative Ulster: Marking Punk's Bangor Birthplace." *BBC News,* September 10, 2018. Available at https://www.bbc.com/news/uk-northern-ireland-45317415. Accessed September 25, 2024.

Graham, Bill. "Interview with Jake Burns of Stiff Little Fingers." *Hot Press*, 1982. Available at https://www.hotpress.com/music /happy-birthday-jake-burns-read-a-1982-interview-with-stiff -little-fingers-frontman-23009754. Accessed October 11, 2024.

Grossberg, Lawrence. *We Gotta Get Out of This Place: Popular Conservatism and Post Modern Culture*. New York/London: Routledge, 1992.

Hebdige, Dick. *Subculture: The Meaning of Style*. London: Routledge, 1979.

Heron, Timothy A. "Alternative Ulster: How Punk Took on the Troubles." *Irish Times*, December 2, 2016. http://irishtimes .com/culture/books/alternative-ulster-how punk-took-on-the-troubles-1.2890644. Accessed January 29, 2019.

Heron, Timothy A. "'Alternative Ulster': The First Wave of Punk in Northern Ireland (1976-1983)." In *Made in Ireland: Studies in Popular Music*, edited by Áine Mangaoang, John O'Flynn, and Lonán Ó Briain. London: Routledge, 2020.

Hesmondhalgh, David. "Post-Punk's Attempt to Democratize the Music Industry: The Success and Failure of Rough Trade." *Popular Music* 16, no. 3 (1997): 255–74.

Hooley, Terri and Richard Sullivan. *Hooleygan: Music, Mayhem, Good Vibrations*. Belfast: Blackstaff Press, 2010.

Hooley, Terri, interview with author, March 4, 2019.

Jones, Helen. "Teenage Kicks mural reinstated in Belfast after Outcry." *BBC News*, March 16, 2015. Available at https://www .bbc.com/news/uk-northern-ireland-31909136. Accessed September 15, 2024.

Kinzer, P.J. "Northern Irish Punks Protex Get Ready for Their Nashville Debut." *Nashville Scene*, March 6, 2024. Available at https://www.nashvillescene.com/music/features/protex-aidan -murtagh-interview-northern-ireland-punk-eastside-bowl

-nashville/article_69685774-da83-11ee-934e-439df339bf24
.html. Accessed September 30, 2024.

Link, Roland. *Kicking Up A Racket: The Story of Stiff Little Fingers 1977-1983*. Belfast: Appletree, 2009.

Mallie, Eamonn and Patrick Bishop. *The Provisional IRA*. London: Heinemann, 1987.

Marcus, Greil. *Lipstick Traces: A Secret History of the Twentieth Century*. Cambridge, MA: Harvard University Press, 1989.

Martin, Gavin. "Northern Ireland: The Fantasy and The Reality." *New Musical Express*, October 11, 1980, 31–4, 61.

McCann. Fionna. "'Special Powers' in the North of Ireland: Abuse, Repression, and Resistance." *The Funambulist* #29 (April 2020): 50–3. Available at https://thefunambulist.net/magazine /states-of-emergency/special-powers-in-the-north-of-ireland -abuse-repression-and-resistance-by-fiona-mccann. Accessed September 4, 2024.

McCullough, Dave (aka "D. Angry"). "LAMF." *Alternative Ulster* 72 (1978): 2.

McLoone, Martin. "Punk Music in Northern Ireland." *Irish Studies Review* 12, no. 1 (2004): 29–8.

Melaugh, Martin. "Estimates of the Strength of Paramilitary Groups." Ulster University's CAIN [Conflict Archive on the Internet] Project, n.d. Available at https://cain.ulster.ac.uk/ issues/violence/paramilitary2.htm. Accessed September 5, 2024.

Melucci, Alberto. *Nomads of the Present: Social Movements and Individual Needs in Contemporary Society*. Philadelphia: Temple University Press, 1989.

Middles, Mick. "Stiff Little Fingers: The Voice Squad." *Sounds*, March 1, 1980.

Moody, T.W. and F.X. Martin, eds. *The Course of Irish History*, 5th edition. Lanham, MD: Rinehart, 2012.

Morley, Paul. "Belfast's Ripped Back Sides." *New Musical Express,* February 17, 1979.

Morley, Paul. "Review of Stiff Little Fingers' Inflammable Material." *New Musical Express,* February 10, 1979.

Moynahan, Julian. *Anglo-Irish: The Literary Imagination in a Hyphenated Culture.* Princeton: Princeton University Press, 1995.

Myers, Kevin. *Watching the Door: Cheating Death in 1970s.* Belfast. Atlantic Books, 2008.

Northern Ireland General Register Office. "Census of Population 1971, Religious Tables, Northern Ireland." Available at https:// www.nisra.gov.uk/sites/nisra.gov.uk/files/publications/1971 -census-religion-tables.PDF. Accessed July 18, 2024.

Northern Visions NVTV. "Giro's." Documentary. April 16, 2010. Available at https://vimeo.com/10976273. Accessed August 16, 2019.

O'Neil, Sean and Guy Trelford. *It Makes You Want to Spit!: The Definitive Guide to Punk in Northern Ireland 1977-1982.* Dublin: Reekus Music, 2003.

Rachel, Daniel. *Walls Come Tumbling Down: Rock Against Racism, 2 Tone, Red Wedge.* London: Picador, 2017.

Roulston, Fearghus. *Belfast Punk and The Troubles: An Oral History.* Manchester: Manchester University Press, 2022.

Ryder, Chris. *The RUC, 1922–1997: A Force under Fire,* 3rd rev. edition. London: Random House, 1997.

Silverton, Peter. "Stiff Little Fingers: Profile and Interview." *Sounds,* October 7, 1978.

Specia, Megan and Ed O'Loughlin. "Catholics Outnumber Protestants in Norther Ireland for the First Time." *The New York Times,* September 22, 2022.

Statista. "Total Number of Deaths per Year During the Troubles (the Northern Ireland Conflict) from 1969 to 2001." n.d.

Available at https://www.statista.com/statistics/1401907/ni
-troubles-deaths-annual/. Accessed September 15, 2024.

Stewart, Francis. "Alternative Ulster: Punk Rock as a Means of
Overcoming Religious Divide in Northern Ireland." In *Irish
Religious Conflict in Comparative Perspective*, edited by John
Wolffe. Basingstoke: Palgrave Macmillan, 2014.

Stewart, Tony. "It's a Dog's Life in Today's Belfast." *New Musical
Express,* March 25, 1978, 11.

Street, John. *Rebel Rock: The Politics of Popular Music.* Oxford:
Basil Blackwell, 1986.

Ulster TV. "It Makes You Want To Spit." Documentary,
1978. Available at https://youtu.be/mnPmE-q4jS8?si
=luJCAxEe8HsvUEhl. Accessed 3 October 2024.

Weitzer, Ronald. *Policing Under Fire: Ethnic Conflict and Police-
Community Relations in Northern Ireland.* Albany: SUNY Press,
1995.

Xvx, Mittens. "The Story of the Warzone Collective." 2014.
Available at https://diyconspiracy.net/the-warzone-collective/.
Accessed September 5, 2019.

Young, Brian, interview with author, March 5, 2019.